GAME PLAN

Developing Intentional Missional Ministry

Tim Roehl

1865919915 3

Game Plan: Developing Intentional Missional Ministry

Originally published as *Game Plan: Developing Intentional Missional Ministry*
Copyright © 2012, The Wesleyan Church. Used by permission.

ISBN: 978-1-51177-839-8

Revised and Updated Copyright © 2015, 2016 by Tim Roehl

For more information and resources:
Game Plan worksheets: timroehl.net/home/game-plan
Coaching Tips videos: timroehl.net/home/coaching-tips-videos
Facebook: www.facebook.com/gameplanresources
Email: TimRoehl@usfamily.net

GAME PLAN

Developing Intentional Missional Ministry

What Others Say About Game Plan

"It gives me great pleasure to endorse this edition of Dr. Tim Roehl's book. Having served with Tim in denominational settings and now as fellow missionaries with One Mission Society, I can say unequivocally that what Tim says he lives. Both our denomination and the mission have experienced significant growth as a result of Dr. Tim's leadership and guidance. You will find *Game Plan* to be a virtual gold mine of material presented in a clear and very readable manner. The small size and the engaging story/case study method of presentation allows the reader to be ushered into this coaching setting and soon swept into wanting to have your own 'Bill' coach and make the discoveries and enjoy the experiences that 'Tom' is having. And if the reader will thoughtfully and prayerful enter into the exercises on 'Coaching Yourself Forward,' he/she will be involved in missional ministry. While this book is written out of Dr. Roehl's experience and expertise, he shares materials from many other pathfinders and provides a brief selective bibliography of very helpful works at the end of each major section. As good as these are the appendices make the book a resource that you will return to frequently. Dr. Roehl's desire is to equip and release the reader for missional ministry. I highly commend the book to you regardless of the stage of ministry in which you are involved. Come enjoy the journey to being all God wants you to be."
—The Rev. Dr. William H Vermillion, PhD
Vice President of Theological Education, One Mission Society
Former General Superintendent of the Evangelical Church, 2002-2006

"As a district superintendent, I highly recommend Dr. Tim Roehl's revised version of *Game Plan: Developing Intentional Missional Ministry*. Dr. Roehl is not only an outstanding coach, he combines effective pastoral and church planting experience with extremely insightful and practical helps for helping pastors lead their congregations in missional ministry. He is a must read for any pastor serious about transforming lives and communities."
—Dr. Aron P. Willis
District Superintendent, Indiana North District, The Wesleyan Church

"I love the story Tim uses to get across his message. It captures your attention and makes the development of missional ministry come alive through the characters Tim has developed. He makes it a very practical, step by step process without it feeling like it. For me what makes his message even more tangible, is having had him for a coach myself. Tim isn't just writing a book—he is sharing his heart for developing people and changing lives. This is the real thing and so is he."
—Rev. Ray Van Gilst
District Superintendent, Christian and Missionary Alliance, Central Pacific District

"This book you hold in your hand is a very practical and biblical approach to helping local church leaders move their congregations from missional miss to biblical obedience and fruitfulness. Tim is a good friend who practices what he preaches and writes. This material is not borne out of a laboratory absent of real congregational life. This book is borne from real life with real life application. It has the potential of radically changing you and your congregation with a strategic plan that will honor God, reach the broken, hurting and lost and grow up believers into to Christ like followers. You will not be disappointed!"
—Dr. Dan A. Berry
District Superintendent, South Coastal District, The Wesleyan Church
Author of *No More Cloudy Days; The Bend in the Road is not the End of the Road*

"Tim Roehl and I share similar values, especially empowering others to lead through coaching and finding creative ways to bring Jesus to our world. In *Game Plan*, Tim equips us to coach others through the story of two leaders on a coaching journey. He also equips ministry leaders with a pathway to develop their own unique, practical and biblical game plan for missional ministry. As you read the principles and practices of *Game Plan*, you'll find the keys to discern and develop your own game plan for ministry...and learn how to coach others to do the same. I'm glad to recommend *Game Plan*!"
—Dan Reiland
Executive Pastor, 12Stone Church, Atlanta, Georgia

"Reading Tim's updated version of *Game Plan* took me back to my early days of ministry. I was big on vision and small on strategy. Tim came alongside of me then as he does today. He coached me to turn my vision into strategy into reality. He writes as a player/coach having experience on both the field and the sideline."
—Rev. D. Keith Dickerson
Pastor, Hope Community Church of Lake Oswego, Oregon
CEO, Lake Oswego Chamber of Commerce

"Tim Roehl masterfully accomplishes his goal to create a 'coach yourself forward' resource manual! His questions for personal self-reflection or team discussion stimulate vision and discernment and the appendices provide biblically-based missional strategies rich with application...all this in a book that is highly engaging and adaptable to the reader's own pace."
—Dr. Wayne Schmidt
Vice President, Wesley Seminary, Indiana Wesleyan University

"Practical! Practical! Practical! The narrative approach and breadth of resources make *Game Plan* a must-have, practical resource for engaging the Great Commission in meaningful, missional ways. Every lay person, pastor, missionary and church planter who is serious about making disciples will find this to be a useful resource. This is a book to order by the case to share with others in your personal efforts to make and multiply disciples."
—Rev. Bob Ransom
US Ministries Director, The Missionary Church

"*Game Plan* is not for cowardly leaders who wish to play it safe. It is for those brave souls who are willing to get out of the bubble of 'doing church as usual' in order to make a difference in their community and beyond. You will find this self-coaching guide practical and relevant for creating a missional culture in your church."
—Mark O. Wilson
Pastor, Author of *Purple Fish* and *Filled Up, Poured Out*

"This book is a significant resource. With its intentionality, strategic thinking, along with its action plans and combined with its narrative style, this book is a 'must have' for all those involved in ministry and who wish to see the Great Commission fulfilled in this generation."
—Rev. Stephen Williamson
Ireland Field Director, One Mission Society

"I greatly appreciate *Game Plan* for us in working with missionary development in the Caribbean. I was looking for a practical guide for ministry development for any context and I found it in *Game Plan*. Since it is practical and biblically-based, it is well received and useful across cultures. Since it has a story line, it is easy to follow in a practical way."
—Richard Yoder
Caribbean Field Director, One Mission Society

"*Game Plan* is a game changer. The coach approach in every chapter allows readers to immediately develop a community impacting *Game Plan*. If you desire to reach a community for Christ, this book will prove to be more valuable than any seminar you have ever attended."
—Sam Farina
Coaching Task Force Leader, Assemblies of God USA

"*Game Plan* is a must read for anyone struggling to make sense of church life or who longs to fit and flourish in God's kingdom. Tim Roehl provides a delicate balance of coaching, coach training and clear and helpful teaching. It was easy to follow the conversation Roehl provides, replacing Tom's name with my name. His story overlaps my story. Maybe yours as well. Having first-hand exposure to Tim and his coaching and teaching ministry, *Game Plan* is about as close as you can get without flying him in for the weekend. It's an easy read. But you will want to linger over each section until it becomes yours. Read it. Read it with others."
—Rev. Les Cool
Pastor, Director of Church Planting, Evangelical Congregational Church

"What a joy to find a road map with 'next steps' to encourage building Great Commission churches through Great Commandment living. *Game Plan* achieves this well."
—Dr. Gary E. Wright
President, World Renewal International
Evangelist, Evangelical Friends Church; Community Church Missions

"Moving into missional ministry has practical implications for individual believers, church leaders, pastors and denominational leaders. My friend Tim's book provides practical insight into the

meaning of missional ministry and helps people understand how they can live and serve missionally in every aspect of life."
—Rev. Dr. Ron Hamilton
National Conference Minister, Conservative Congregational Christian Conference

"Tim and I lived this book together when he coached me as a church planter! As a seasoned 'player-coach,' Tim combines decades of personal experience and cutting-edge research to bring us this practical handbook on becoming Christ-empowered missional Christians who will lead God's Church to reach the hearts and lives of people everywhere. Tim taps into the very heartbeat of God, as he brings tangible insight on how to become disciples who make up disciple-making, missional churches. A MUST READ for all growing Christ followers and church leaders!"
—Dr. Tom Heins
Director of Church Planting, Pacific Conference of The Evangelical Church

"Most pastors I know are struggling just to keep their congregations happy. We all want to reach the lost but we spend most of our energy simply meeting members' expectations. Many of us grab a book or attend a conference to discover the 'secret' to turning our churches around. This prepackaged approach is hopeless. Tim Roehl challenges us to do the hard work of seeking God's plan for turning our congregations into teams of missionaries sent out to reach our communities. This is spiritually and strategically strenuous but extremely rewarding. Lives are transformed. Members become ministers. Unbelievers become committed followers of Christ. By God's grace, the Spirit is rewriting my church's DNA. He will do it in you and your church too. Start seeking the Spirit's *Game Plan* today."
—Rev. Mark Haines
Pastor, Bay City Wesleyan Church, Bay City, Michigan

"*Game Plan* is a great resource for church planters of all kinds. Tim Roehl has put together tremendous guidelines that help pastors in all aspects of leading a church. He used them when he coached me as a church planter. I found this book extremely helpful in refreshing areas that I have left alone. It also helped me do some personal evaluation of my spiritual journey which challenged me to allow

Jesus to provide fresh creativity in my soul and His ministry. Use *Game Plan* to help start your church, define your church and refresh your church. This also needs to be in schools and seminaries for training future Christian leaders. Thanks, Tim!"
—Rev. Jon Strutz
Pastor Mountain View Community Church, Oregon City, Oregon

"Tim Roehl takes his role as coach seriously and that's a good thing for readers of *Game Plan!* By combining story, solid coaching questions, meaningful statistics, useful tools and an accountability to action, Tim coaches his readers toward a new kind of ministry understanding and a more accountable kind of ministry activity. If you coach yourself to new actions because of your *Game Plan,* you'll make a new and meaningful contribution to God's kingdom! I hope you do!"
—Jonathan Reitz
Director of Training/CEO CoachNet Global, www.coachnet.org

"*Game Plan* is truly just as the title says it is. In order to engage a community with the Gospel of Jesus there must be an intentional way to do it. Tim Roehl takes you step by step in developing a strategy to become a church that is relevant to your community. This book has helped our leaders understand what it means to be on mission with God. The results have been overwhelming. As a lead pastor, I recommend this book to any church that is seeking to make a difference."
—Rev. Edgar Rodriguez
Lead pastor, New Hope Church, Moville, Iowa
Chaplain, Woodbury County Sheriff's Department

"*Game Plan* is a must read for anyone desiring to learn the 'how-to's' for developing a missional ministry. Creatively written from a coaching perspective with both the spiritual and strategic in view, Tim gleans from years of ministry experience as a pastor, church planter, ministry coach, leader of leaders and author. Whether you're beginning or transitioning your ministry, Dr. Roehl will guide you through the process of how to be on mission for God!
—Rev. Tim Maki
Pastor, North Star Church, Hibbing, Minnesota
Head of North Star Network

"I speak from experience! We have used *Game Plan* in various forms of church ministry and different points of our journey. Tim's authentic heart for all expressions of the Church and lost people is wonderfully conveyed in *Game Plan*. It both challenges and equips the mindset/heartset of 100-year-old established churches or church plants, thriving churches or churches in decline, individuals or small groups. Unlike many books that will stay on your bookshelf, *Game Plan* offers practical, hands-on help as you engage your communities. We are using these principles as we engage Marshalltown and plant a new church. Thank you for pouring into us!"
—Rev. Dylan Does
Pastor Restore Church, Marshalltown, Iowa

"Tim Roehl has always irritated me—like an oyster is irritated by a grain of sand in the process of making a pearl. In oft creative and thoughtful ways, he calls me and us to join him in playing our parts in reaching the world for Christ through our churches and ministries. But *Game Plan* takes such an endeavor to a new level, necessary because of the new and ever shifting, changing world around us. Tim's coaching approach enables leaders to understand how who they are fits into God's wider, deeper plan to reach the world...beginning right next door. It gives them practical ways and means to involve others in their church or ministry or small group to do the same—often together. He even provides simple ways and means to understand those whom you are trying to reach! Let me personalize this. Tim encourages me to think creatively in the 'how' and the 'who' for reaching those around me in my relational connecting, in using my own gifts and even to contextualize the message of the Gospel in fun ways. He also encourages me to strategize with those I engage or train on these issues in a more systematic and creative ways than I would have on my own. I found myself already challenged to think outside the box in the preface! He holds us accountable to taking active, specific and guided steps in doing so; something that really helps me. I believe it will help you as well. Believe Tim as he challenges you to look with 'cross-cultural eyes and strategies' about your very own mission field. He and Shirley live out this book in their mission

field, whether next door or halfway around the world with church planters and leaders in other cultures."
—Dr. Paul Ford
Church Resource Ministries Missionary
Author of *Your Leadership Grip, Knocking Over the Leadership Ladder, Moving from I to We*

"As someone who was coached by Tim for three years, many memories as well as challenges were brought back to me as I read through *Game Plan*. Dr. Roehl did not write a how-to book; he just wrote a book from his life experiences on how he has seen God use coaching to help those in the ministry to be more intentionally missional. As I read *Game Plan* I remembered many similar conversations and was reminded why the church I pastor has the missional DNA it does and much of that came from walking my church planting journey with Dr. Roehl. This book will challenge you to break the mold of just doing church to actually being the church in your community for the sake of the Kingdom."
—Jeff Wolheter
Pastor, Bridgeway Evangelical Church, Kendallville, Indiana

"Warning! If you don't care about lost people, don't read this book! Tim Roehl's passion is convicting and contagious. Based on biblical principles that are adaptable to any setting, Game Plan: Developing Intentional Missional Ministry will change you, your church and your community. If you live it, they will come!"
Pastor David Dignal
Director of Church Health, Indiana North District, The Wesleyan Church

"As a young pastor in the 1950s, I was always looking for resources to improve my ministry. When I saw Tim Roehl's *Game Plan*, I instantly knew this was something that would have made a world of difference to a young pastor. I can only hope that both beginning and maturing pastors will see in this book, the very thing that will add tremendous value to their life and ministry. By all means buy and use this *Game Plan*. "
—Daniel E. Finch
Retired Wesleyan Church pastor, denominational leader
Author of *Transfusion*

"In *Game Plan*, Tim Roehl has masterfully outlined a path for missional church practitioners to not only craft a ministry vision, but develop a plan that supports the leader's desired cultural ethos. In a unique way, Roehl begins and ends with Jesus' vision for the Church. Leaders will discover relevant ministry ideas and many time-tested resources. *Game Plan* is not only worth the read—it is the type of resource leaders will want to pass on to their teammates!"

—Dr. Ed Love

Pastor, Coach and Professor of Church Multiplication, Wesley Biblical Seminary, Marion, Indiana

Foreword

Do you or your church need a new game plan? Have your current ministries lost their steam? Is it becoming more difficult to reach lost people and make disciples? The attractional ministry methods of the last three decades are not as effective as they used to be. Many Christian leaders have discovered the need to become missionaries to their culture and not just shepherds to the flock. If they are not coming to us, then we must take the Gospel to them in word, deed and power so that they might experience Jesus.

However, many of us have never been equipped to do that, and our churches are not organized to that end or focused on that priority. Most churches are better suited to help believers be disciples rather than helping lost people become disciples. Ninety percent of our ministry activity is focused on believers.

Tim Roehl helps us develop a new game plan to help us reach lost people and make new disciples. The new game plan helps us realign our vision with Christ's mission to seek and to save the lost. The new game plan helps us understand the mission field in our own city, country and the world. The new game plan helps us meet needs and communicate the Gospel in a secular culture. The new game plan helps us re-align our ministries so that we actually achieve God's mission for the church as stated in the Great Commission in Matthew 28. The new game plan will take time to work out in your life or your church. Do not expect a quick fix or easy answers.

Tim and I have been friends and ministry teammates for many years. We've equipped thousands of leaders in the principles and practices of coaching and missional ministry. This book is the distilled wisdom of working with leaders from many nations, denominations and mission agencies. Tim offers an easy-to-read style as most of the principles are presented through conversations between a pastor and his coach.

Whether you are planting a church, leading an existing church into more intentional missional ministry or bringing Jesus to your mission field anywhere in the world, you'll find *Game Plan* an enjoyable and practical read. I recommend it to you. Get started today!

Dr. Steve Ogne
Coach, Trainer, Author, Consultant
Co-author, *TransforMissional Coaching*
steve@steveogne.org

Preface

My friend Jeff's voice had a note of uncertainty. "Man," he said, "I know what to do when I've got people, but I don't know what to do when I don't. What do I do?"

Jeff had been a terrific youth pastor in a larger church, but now as a church planter in a new community, he was learning an uncomfortably common reality: many church leaders know how to "do church," but struggle to make disciples and gather people as a missionary. As his coach, I encouraged him that what he was feeling wasn't unusual and said we'd have to shift from church leader to missionary. The Lord had brought him to his new city on purpose...there was a mission field of people longing for God, waiting for someone like him and his team to help them find and follow Him!

"Great," Jeff said. "How do we do that?"

That's the essential question. Living in a culture that has shifted dramatically in recent decades, ministry must be treated as cross-cultural missions more than ever. How to make the shift from traditional church leader to missional leader is a defining issue in our day.

From that question forward, I coached Jeff to develop a game plan to approach his city and church planting ministry as a missionary. It was different than what he was used to, but as each step unfolded Jeff could see how the Lord was going ahead of him, preparing the way for their team to be and bring the Good News of Jesus. Even before they officially launched as a church they were known by leaders of influence across the city as a group that wanted to serve and bless their community. Now, several years later, hundreds of people have come to know Christ, the church continues to be highly regarded and they are starting ministries in new locations. Jeff has truly made the shift from church leader to missionary to missional leader of a missional church.

In my own ministry journey, I've had the privilege of growing up going to a traditional church in a small town, being part of starting a church as a teenager; restarting a church in the heart of a large urban "heart of the city" setting; planting a church in a growing suburban environment; and being a denominational leader equipping new and existing church leaders to start and strengthen churches to reach more people for Christ. I also had the joy of being a missionary based in North America, leading a team that focused on assessing, coaching and training leaders who serve in many denominations and nations across North America and around the world. I now serve as a leader in a mission agency that minsters in over 75 nations. However, my wife and I see our own neighborhood as our primary mission field...loving people next door as well as equipping leaders around the world is my context.

Take off our organizational labels, and you'll find growing numbers of leaders united by a common passion to bring the Good News of Jesus to people and communities who don't know Him yet. The issues leaders face are universal. Until recent years, the majority of church planters and pastors were trained to focus their efforts on doing church better by trying to develop services and programs that will attract people to come to them. However, the Holy Spirit has been increasingly calling His leaders out of their church buildings and programs and out into their mission fields. The term "missional" is now a familiar term in ministry circles. We are learning to think, pray, go and act as missionaries in wonderful ways. Fueled by a passion for people and communities who don't yet know the transforming, powerful love of Jesus and guided by the purifying power and creative wisdom of the Holy Spirit, leaders are developing ministry starting with the needs and opportunities of their mission field, more than just relying on a particular method or style of doing church.

I've had the privilege of assessing, training and coaching thousands leaders who long to bring Jesus to their world. As I coach leaders, one of the consistent areas we work on is developing a game plan to become great missionaries to their mission field. For most leaders, it requires a shift in priorities and activities that at first are uncomfortable, but later become more fruitful than they could have imagined. Seeing people come to Christ fuels our passion and helps us overcome our obstacles!

This resource is a compilation of coaching conversations, training opportunities and ministry experiences I've had with thousands of leaders. I've benefited from the wisdom of many leaders, some who I can acknowledge in these pages. Others I can't recognize with a "footnote" because I've forgotten where I've heard an important truth or ministry tip, but I do remember the power of the insight that was imprinted on my heart and mind.

Game Plan: Developing Intentional Missional Ministry is both a book and a "coach yourself forward" resource manual. It's designed to help you develop a game plan for missional ministry that is both spiritual and strategic, whether you lead in a new or existing church. The principles and practics of *Game Plan* are designed for you to adapt to your unique setting, trusting the Holy Spirit to give you the authority, anointing and wisdom to bring the Good News to your mission field. We'll help you become more intentional, missional and accountable in your ministry by highlighting biblical principles and practical ideas. Each section of this resource will include conversations between two leaders that illustrate the power of coaching and the essential issues we face as leaders. There will be practical "nuts and bolts" tools to help you discover and apply the insights and skills to your mission field. "Coach yourself forward" questions will guide you to your own game plan. We'll also suggest further resources that will help you go deeper.

When I originally wrote *Game Plan*, I had North American leaders in mind. However, in developing ministry equipping materials over the years, I have consciously tried to be more "biblical and universal" than just "North American and evangelical"—in other words, I wanted biblical principles that would work anywhere in the world, not just in a North American context. I wondered how well the principles and practical skills of Game Plan would work in other nations and cultures. As a missionary with One Mission Society (OMS), I get to work with leaders from over 75 nations. To my delight, leaders from other countries are affirming and asking for copies of *Game Plan*, often telling me, "This will help us…this is just what we need." In addition, we are seeing the nations come to North America, giving us unprecedented opportunities to be missionaries in wonderful ways both "across the street and around the world."

We're praying with you that as you go and sow, the Lord of the Harvest will supernaturally make things grow!

Let's develop a game plan to bring Jesus to your mission field! They're waiting and ready…let's go!

Tim Roehl

The Journey Begins...

"Nice sermon, Pastor. I wish my neighbor could have heard that...he really needs it."

Al Johnson's grip was firm, his look sincere. Tom smiled back at him in return. "Thanks, Al, I appreciate it. Hope to see your neighbor here with you soon."

Al shook his head slightly as he replied, "I'm trying, Pastor, but he doesn't seem all that interested in church. I wish we could bring Jesus to him so he could understand how much the Lord loves him... Well, have a good day. Thanks again for a good message."

Tom continued shaking hands and greeting people, but Al's simple statement stuck to his heart. *"I wish we could bring Jesus to him so he could understand how much the Lord loves him..."* It was the same feeling he'd been having, too. It was more than a feeling, though...it was a growing longing.

Tom's church was doing all right in many ways. It had the ministries most churches have for their own families. Yet, he found himself dealing with many common frustrations other pastors deal with. Conversations with his network of friends spread out around the country and the world, each trying to serve Christ in their respective environments, confirmed similar issues. All of them were trying to meet people's expectations in the church and those expectations were as many and varied as people's preferences. Each, however, confessed to a growing sense of urgency about how many people were without Christ all around them. Somehow in the midst of all the "regular" tasks of church leadership there seemed to be little time for ministry out in their communities. Tom's church had lots of activity, but lacked a compelling focus and passion. They didn't have the kind of influence for Christ that would consistently bring people to know Jesus and see real transformation of individuals, families and entire communities.

"I wish we could bring Jesus to him..." Yes, Al had captured clearly what Tom had been thinking and praying about...

> *"I wish we could bring Jesus to him so he could understand how much the Lord loves him..."*

not just bringing church to people, but bringing Jesus to his community. But how?

The lobby was almost empty now as people headed out to Sunday lunch. Tom's wife was finishing up a visit with one of her friends, giving him the signal that she'd soon be ready for their family to head home for their lunch waiting in the slow cooker. Off to his right, Tom noticed Bill was praying with one of the newer men in their church who had started coming with Bill recently. Bill and his family were back from an overseas missionary assignment for a few months before beginning another term. Although this was Bill's home church, Tom didn't know him well because he'd begun his ministry while Bill and his family were still overseas. What Tom had heard about Bill made him want to know him better, though. In a country many considered spiritually resistant and nearly unreachable, Bill had been the catalyst to equip leaders who were planting churches and reaching people for Christ in amazing numbers. Whatever Bill was doing, it was working.

Walking toward him, Bill extended his hand with a warm smile. "Good word today, Pastor," he said.

"Thanks," Tom said smiling back. "Coming from a fellow minister, that means a lot."

"Well, we missionaries need to encourage each other all we can, with the size of the mission we've been given," returned Bill.

"Hey, you're the missionary," joked Tom. "I'm just a pastor."

Bill looked at him steadily for a moment before speaking. His tone was quiet but earnest. "We're all missionaries, friend. No matter where we serve, people's hearts and our mission is still the same." He paused and smiled again. "Hey, I'd like to get together and hear more of what God's up to around here. Got time for coffee?"

Tom nodded. "Thanks, I'd love to. I want to hear more about what God's been doing through your ministry, too. How about lunch on Tuesday? I'll buy."

"Works for me. How about noon at that diner on Walnut just off Main? Love the home cooking and the prices." Pulling out their smart phones and inputting the information, they confirmed the meeting.

Tom didn't know it then, but it was the first of a series of conversations that would forever change his own leadership journey, the ministry of his church, his community and his influence with other leaders.

"Seeing"

Through the Father's Eyes

Tuesday noon found Tom and Bill at the diner, greeting each other with the easy familiarity of men who share the common ground of ministry.

"I appreciate you meeting with me, Tom," said Bill. "Even though God's call has taken me a long way from here, I still pray often for my home church and for you. I've been looking forward to getting to know you better."

"I've been looking forward to getting to know you better, too," replied Tom. "What I hear about what the Lord is doing through your ministry is pretty amazing. I'd love to know more about what you've done to see the results you are getting."

Bill smiled. "I'd be glad to talk ministry, but first I want to learn more about you, your family and your ministry journey. What's your story?"

"Ok, I'll tell you my story if you'll tell me yours," Tom smiled back in return.

"Sounds good...you first." With that, Bill leaned forward slightly with a look that said, "I'm listening...what you have to say is important to me."

Tom found himself sharing his story easily as Bill listened intently, occasionally nodding and graciously asking questions that opened doors for Tom to share even more. As he related how God had worked through the experiences and people of his life, Tom sensed a deep reaffirmation of the Lord's call for him. He found himself sharing with Bill some of his greatest joys, challenges and longings to fulfill the call Christ had on his life and church, including his thoughts about bringing Jesus to their community from the previous Sunday. Even though Bill didn't say much, his ministry of listening was a powerful gift to Tom. Finally, Tom leaned back in his chair and grinned sheepishly. "Wow. I didn't intend on sharing all that! Thanks for listening."

"Glad to," replied Bill. "You've got quite a story. It sounds like Jesus has really been speaking to you in some deep ways, especially in your desire to bring His love through our church to our community. Like I said Sunday, we're all missionaries. I can tell you are on the way to overcoming some of the biggest obstacles I've had to overcome in my ministry."

"Thanks," Tom said. "I think I'm beginning to understand what you mean about being a missionary a bit better. You said you had to overcome some big obstacles. What are they?"

"Before I share them with you, could I share part of my story?" Bill replied. "I had an experience that forever changed some things for me, especially how I view my mission."

Now Tom leaned forward to listen. "Please," he said. "Tell me more."

Bill looked down for a moment and when he looked up again it was as if he was looking back in time, reliving a signature event in his life. "Well," he said, "it happened a number of years ago when my brother, Dad and I were deer hunting. I still regard that day as one of the most frightening times in my life. We were eleven miles out in the middle of nowhere...miles beyond the paved roads, gravel roads and even off the muddy, rutted logging roads in the midst of the large forest where we hunted every fall. Our deer stands were scattered out in those deep woods along faint game trails in the midst of birch, pine and maple trees, carpeted with dense, bushy undergrowth. Those woods went for miles...make a wrong turn and a man could be lost for a long time. Being lost in those woods could have deadly consequences. One cold day my brother got lost as evening descended. I heard Randy call to me from the increasing darkness, a note of uncertainty in his voice... 'Bill?' I called back to him, urgency in mine. 'Randy, I'm over here!' Walking toward his voice, we called to each other for a long time, until he saw my waving flashlight and we found each other. He was exhausted from trying to find his way in the dark boggy under-brush. I nearly carried him, our rifles and backpacks out of the woods to our hunting cabin where our father anxiously waited. I'll never forget my Dad's call across the dark meadow as we came toward him... 'Are there one...or two?' I called back, 'We're both here!' Later, after Randy collapsed exhausted into bed, my Dad said to me, 'I'm sure glad you went back in after him.' My response without even thinking was, 'I wasn't coming back without him.'"

Bill stopped and looked at Tom, eyes moist, the look on his face showing the evidence of how deeply the experience still affected him. "Tom, the words 'lost' and 'found' have never been the same to me since. As I've thought about that night, I realized that life got very simple when my brother's life was at stake. My mission became singularly clear. Nothing else mattered but finding my brother and bringing him home safely. Now I really understand what Jesus meant when He said that He came to seek and save the lost. Everything's been different since, especially in how I view ministry."

"Life got very simple when my brother's life was at stake. My mission became singularly clear."

The two men sat silently in the significance of what Bill had shared. In that silence, the Spirit of God spoke to Tom, fueling passion for lost people deep within him, sharpening his sense of call into a singular mission.

Bill spoke quietly again. "I can tell you more of my story and our ministry, but everything I am and do comes from what the Lord imprinted on my heart that night about seeking the lost. That one central passion defines and fuels my mission. As ministry leaders, there are many things we could do, but there is one thing we must do. That's what helped me overcome those obstacles I talked about before."

Tom nodded in understanding. "Thank you. What you shared is clarifying some things for me, too. I'm afraid I've been too scattered and vague about my sense of mission. It shows in our church, too. I haven't had the urgency about lost people that I need. The Lord and I have some things to work through about that. You mentioned that you had to overcome some obstacles. What were they?"

"There were two main obstacles," Bill said. "First, I realized that I was more in love with a particular model of ministry than I was burdened for the lost people in my mission field. Second, I knew how to 'do church' but I didn't know how to think and act as a missionary. I'd allowed myself to live with those barriers, somehow considering them acceptable excuses for too much 'church as usual' ministry. But when the Lord gave me a holy urgency for lost people, I couldn't let them hinder me anymore. Everything had to be about making disciples who made disciples who made disciples and multiplying new communities of faith. I had to change the way I approached ministry. It wasn't easy, but...it's been worth it."

"You're not the only one with those obstacles," Tom admitted. "That's my current reality. But how can I overcome them? I want that holy urgency you talked about. I want to see a continual stream of lost people coming to Christ. I want to make disciples who make disciples. I want to see the Lord use our church to see real transformation in our community...our mission field." He looked at Bill, his face a mix of desperation and determination. "Would you be willing to walk with me...help me? I've been stuck too long. Too many people are lost without Jesus and we've got to do something about that."

"Tom," Bill said, "it would be an honor. If you want, we can meet regularly and see how you can become the lead missionary of a church full of missionaries to our community."

"Thanks, Bill...I'd like that." The two set up a time to meet later that week at a local coffee shop before quietly praying together for each other, those around them in the diner, their church and their mission field.

Main barriers to missional ministry:

1. **Leaders who are more in love with a model than their mission field.**

2. **Leaders who know how to "do church: but don't know how to be a missionary to their community.**

"Holy urgency...lost people." The words echoed in Tom's spirit long after their visit. They became the plea of his heart as he and Jesus talked long into the night.

Our Singular Aspiration...His Mission

Sometimes it takes a dramatically defining experience to focus us on what matters most in life. The defining event of all human history was when Jesus, compelled by His love, left His home in heaven on a rescue mission. Seeking us when we were lost and captive, He literally laid down His life so we could be redeemed, reconciled and restored to a right relationship to our Father. It was His singular mission. His redemptive love and power make transformation possible on personal, family, community and cultural levels.

God's Church is strongest when we focus on the singular mission we've been given. Jesus described His redemptive mission in a number of ways. Read these verses and capture your insights about the scope of His mission.

"Then He added, "now go and learn the meaning of this Scripture: 'I want you to show mercy, not offer sacrifices.' For I have come to call not those who think they are righteous, but those who know they are sinners." (Matthew 9:13 NLT)

"The Son of Man came not to be served but to serve others and to give His life as a ransom for many." (Mark 10:45 NIV)

"The Spirit of the Lord is on me, because He has anointed me to proclaim Good News to the poor. He has sent Me to proclaim freedom for the prisoners and recovery of sight for the blind, to set the oppressed free, to proclaim the year of the Lord's favor." (Luke 4:18-19 NIV)

"The Son of Man has come to seek and save the lost..." (Luke 19:10 NIV)

"For God loved the world so much that he gave His one and only Son, so that everyone who believes in Him will not perish but have eternal life. God sent his Son into the world not to judge the world, but to save the world through Him." (John 3:16-17 NLT)

"The thief comes only to steal and destroy, but I have come to give them life and have it abundantly." (John 10:10 ESV)

"Then Jesus came to them and said, 'All authority in heaven and on earth has been given to Me. Therefore, go and make disciples of all nations, baptizing them in the name of the Father and of the Son and of the Holy Spirit and teaching them to obey everything I have commanded you. And surely I am with you always, to the very end of the age.'" (Matthew 28:18-20 NIV)

As God's Church, there are many things we might do that are good, but everything must flow from and contribute to the singular mission He's given us: go into our world like He did and make disciples.

When we see our world as our Father does and our hearts are broken by what breaks our Father's heart...

When our hearts are cleansed and filled by holy love and we are led by the Holy Spirit...

When we see the wonder and joy of lives and communities being transformed by Jesus...

Then we experience the fullness of our Father's love and join Him willingly in His redemptive mission.

COACH YOURSELF FORWARD

1. What "defining events" have influenced your heart for lost people?

2. What does the reality of "lost" and "found" mean to you?

3. What keeps you focused and fueled on God's mission? What drains your heart for lost people?

4. What did you learn from the Scripture verses where Jesus described His mission that will influence your church's attitude toward His mission in your community?

5. How could you help your church develop God's heart for lost people?

6. What are the consequences of not making God's redemptive mission a top priority of your ministry?

7. Begin to brainstorm some ways you and your church could join Jesus on His redemptive mission. What ideas come to you at this point?

Passion Meets Authority

When they met again, Tom was eager to share the work that Jesus had been doing in his heart to give him a holy urgency for lost people. "Bill," he said, "what the Lord's been doing in me has been unsettling, uncomfortable and deep. I can't live the same way or do church the same way anymore. The Great Commission has been too often an omission for me and our church...but not anymore. It's going to be primary in all we do. Now when I'm out among people, I find myself wondering how many of them are lost and without Christ...and what it's going to take to reach them. The Lord has ignited something in me. I want to keep that fire burning bright and see my whole church lit up, too."

Bill nodded in understanding affirmation. "You're right... being focused on the harvest and fueled by holy love go hand in glove...you can't have one without the other. I'm glad to hear how you've been thinking differently about the Great Commission. Our great "co-mission" is to join Jesus in making disciples who make disciples who make disciples and multiply new faith communities. That's primary. But, the Lord's also helped me understand some often unnoticed aspects of the Great Commission that have impacted my view of ministry."

"What did you learn that made such a difference?" Tom asked. "We've heard the words of the Great Commission so often that they've become too familiar and easy to skip over."

"There were a few simple truths that transformed my understanding of the Great Commission," Bill said, "But first let me ask you...what's the most important part of the Great Commission to you?"

Tom thought for a moment. "Well," he replied. "The heart of the Great Commission for me is making disciples."

"Good," nodded Bill. "That's the heart of our mission... everything we do must be about making disciples. What changed for me was my attitude about how I was to do that."

"What do you mean?"

"I had been approaching ministry, especially as a missionary, with some assumptions that held me back. My biggest hindrance was that I made God too small and my obstacles too big. I approached ministry from a posture of weakness...that the cultural barriers and spiritual opposition from our enemy were too much to overcome. I expected to lose and so I held back and played it safe. That made it easier to focus on ministry inside the church, instead of going on mission outside our doors."

"Like the ten spies in Numbers 13 who scouted out the land God promised His people but then reported that the giants in the land were so big that the spies looked like grasshoppers?" Tom asked.

"Exactly," nodded Bill. "We are truly in a battle for souls. If we believe we're weak and helpless, we lose the battle before we ever start. The ten spies had that attitude, and because of their influence God's people wandered around for a long time instead of confidently pursuing the mission God gave them."

"Sounds like too many churches today," Tom reflected sadly. "Including mine."

"That's where a holy urgency for lost people made such a difference for me," said Bill. "Like Scripture says in 2 Corinthians 5:14, I became compelled by the love of Christ, but had to change my attitude of weakness that held me back. One day while reading the Great Commission passage some words lit up like I was seeing them for the first time. The truth of those words changed my attitude."

"All authority in heaven and earth have been given to Me... therefore, go... I am with you always..."

"What were they?" Tom leaned forward, listening intently.

"All authority in heaven and earth have been given to Me... therefore, go...I am with you always..." Bill said his face shining. "There it was! Jesus has all authority. He's already won the victory. He's already gone ahead of me and He is sending me with His authority! He's with me! When I understood the spiritual authority we have in Jesus, my attitude changed. I knew there were still battles to fight and obstacles to overcome, but now I realized that I could pray and act from a position of victory, not defeat. For me, understanding spiritual authority has now become the activating power for Great Commission ministry. It was a dimension of the Spirit-filled life I had not really appreciated before. The Holy Spirit can give us love from a pure heart, but I also need His authority and power."

Bill paused and looked at Tom. "What does spiritual authority look like in your life and ministry?"

Tom was silent, the look on his face signaling that the question had touched something unexpected and deep in him. Bill just waited. Finally Tom replied, "That's a really good question. I really haven't given the issue as much attention as I should have. The way you describe it as the key to the Great Commission really makes sense. Now that the Lord's giving me a passion to focus on reaching lost people so we multiply disciples, how do I understand and apply spiritual authority with the attitude you described?

Bill grinned in return. "Good question! Would you like to

focus on that issue for the rest of our conversation today?"

Tom nodded. "Absolutely."

With that focus, their conversation continued with Bill asking questions that helped Tom to get clarity about his understanding of spiritual authority. They looked at passages in Scripture, talked about the theological issues involved and identified some concerns and discoveries about the nature of spiritual authority. Bill invited Tom to generate some options about how he could grow in his understanding of spiritual authority and begin applying those truths to his life and ministry. Before they left, Tom had developed some clear action steps involving further Bible study, resources to read and conversations he would have with others about understanding and activating spiritual authority as leaders and as a church. Tom found himself scribbling discoveries and action steps on a napkin. There was a look of hope in his eyes. This conversation had taken him from discovering a need in his life to developing specific steps to move him forward to address that need!

Bill tapped the notes on the napkin with a smile. "The game plan you've come up with looks really good, Tom," said Bill. "Good job!"

Tom smiled back in return. "Back at you! Whatever you just did sure helped me...thank you!"

"I've had the benefit of having some good coaching and it's really helped me. Coaching was so powerful for me that I decided to learn how to coach others, too. I was using coaching skills in our conversation. I'm glad you found what we did helpful."

"It sure was...keep doing it!" Tom said. "And...could you help me learn how to do that for others? I think these skills will really help me equip my leaders better. When can we meet again?"

"I like the way you're thinking!" Bill said. "Let's set a time for our next visit...and keep me updated on your progress. How about if we pray for each other before we head into the rest of our day?"

The two men prayed, shook hands and headed for their cars. As he drove home, Tom reflected on the discoveries and impact his conversations with Bill were making on him. Not only had the Lord given him clarity and passion about a singular sense of mission, Tom felt his attitude and approach to becoming a Great Commission leader was shifting powerfully. As he silently

Gave thanks, he felt the Holy Spirit whisper to him, "There's more coming, son. I'm with you."

"More, Lord...more please." As Tom's spirit and the Spirit of God continued that conversation, his car became sacred space.

His Spiritual Authority—Our Power

Remember this: it is the Lord of the Harvest who sends us! We go commissioned by the King of the Universe to carry out His purposes, authorized with His power. Many Christians look around them and bemoan how bad things are "out there." When we focus our attention on the disintegration of morality in our society, hostility toward Jesus in cultural media and the visibly increasing activity of Satan, it is easy to be fearful and retreat to the relative safety of hiding behind the walls of our churches and Christian environments. Too often God's people see themselves as weak and unable to engage the world redemptively because people in our culture aren't interested and the spiritual resistance is too strong.

I've heard some say, "Things are so bad...we just can't win." That's a lie! Our focus is in the wrong place. We're listening to the wrong voices. Step back...take another look. Listen again to the longings of people around you. Listen to another Voice and you'll see a different view that energizes you with courage and power.

Here's something most people miss when we talk about the Great Commission: *we focus on the task we've been given, instead of on the resources we have to accomplish the mission.* Think of "commission" as "co-mission." We are on mission *with* Jesus. He starts by reminding us that all authority is His. We have the power of the Holy Spirit filling us and activating His power. That's the oft-forgotten secret of the Great Commission!

The issue of spiritual authority generates much discussion among God's people. Some theological viewpoints tend to ignore it all together, while others carry it to an unbiblical extreme. Because understanding spiritual authority can be controversial, many leaders tend to shy away from it. We can't afford to do that! Our attitude and approach toward applying spiritual authority in our ministries is essential to carrying out the Lord's redemptive mission. Become a student of this issue using John Wesley's four pronged approach. Learn from Scripture, history, reason and experience. This is a vital part of our "on the job training" for missional ministry!

Jesus has all, ultimate authority! The battle's already won. Victory is already secure. Our enemy is a defeated foe. Christ has already gone ahead of us. He's given His power and authority to use wherever He sends us. We can confidently go with Jesus using the supernatural resources He provides!

Go to the Word...

Read these passages from Scripture. What do they teach you about spiritual authority?

"Jesus now called the Twelve and <u>gave them authority and power</u> to deal with all the demons and cure diseases. He commissioned them to preach the news of God's kingdom and heal the sick. He said, 'Don't load yourselves up with equipment. Keep it simple; you are the equipment....' <u>Commissioned</u>, they began their circuit of the villages, preaching the Good News and healing the sick...'" (Luke 9:1-3, 6 MSG, underlining added)

"...<u>I will build My church</u>, a church so expansive with energy that not even the gates of hell will be able to keep it out. And that's not all. <u>I will give you the keys of the kingdom of heaven</u>. You will have complete and free access to God's kingdom, keys to open any and every door: whatever you bind on earth will be bound in heaven and whatever you loose on earth will be loosed in heaven." (Matthew 16:18-19, MSG, underlining added)

"Then Jesus came to them and said, '<u>All authority in heaven and on earth has been given to me. Therefore go</u> and make disciples of all nations, baptizing them in the name of the Father and of the Son and of the Holy Spirit and teaching them to obey everything I have commanded you. <u>I'll be with you as you do this</u>, day after day after day, right up to the end of the age.'" (Matthew 28:18-20 NIV, underlining added)

"For this reason, ever since I heard about your faith in the Lord Jesus and your love for all God's people, I have not stopped giving thanks for you, remembering you in my prayers. I keep asking that the God of our Lord Jesus Christ, the glorious Father, may give you the Spirit of wisdom and revelation, so that you may know Him better. I pray that the eyes of your heart may be enlightened in order that you may know the hope

to which He has called you, the riches of his glorious inheritance in his holy people and <u>his incomparably great power</u> for us who believe. That power is the same as the mighty strength He exerted when he raised Christ from the dead and seated Him at his right hand in the heavenly realms, <u>far above all rule and authority</u>, power and dominion and every name that is invoked, not only in the present age but also in the one to come. And God placed all things under His feet and appointed Him to be head over everything for the church, which is His body, the fullness of Him who fills everything in every way." (Ephesians 1:15-23 NIV, underlining added)

"Finally, <u>be strong in the Lord and in his mighty power</u>. Put on the full armor of God, so that you can take your stand against the devil's schemes. For our struggle is not against flesh and blood, but against the rulers, against the authorities, against the powers of this dark world and against the spiritual forces of evil in the heavenly realms. Therefore put on the full armor of God, so that when the day of evil comes, you may be able to stand your ground and after you have done everything, to stand. Stand firm then, with the belt of truth buckled around your waist, with the breastplate of righteousness in place and with your feet fitted with the readiness that comes from the Gospel of peace. In addition to all this, take up the shield of faith, with which you can extinguish all the flaming arrows of the evil one. Take the helmet of salvation and the sword of the Spirit, which is the word of God. And pray in the Spirit on all occasions with all kinds of prayers and requests. With this in mind, be alert and always keep on praying for all the Lord's people. Pray also for me, that whenever I speak, words may be given me so that I will fearlessly make known the mystery of the Gospel, for which I am an ambassador in chains. Pray that I may declare it fearlessly, as I should." (Ephesians 6:10-20 NIV)

"<u>Therefore God exalted him to the highest place</u> and gave him the name that is above every name, <u>that at the name of Jesus every knee should bow</u>, in heaven and on earth and under the earth, and every tongue acknowledge that Jesus Christ is Lord, to the glory of God the Father." (Philippians 2:9-11 NIV, underlining added)

COACH YOURSELF FORWARD

1. How does Bill and Tom's conversation influence your understanding of the Great Commission?

2. What's your current understanding of spiritual authority? Study the Scripture passages we've listed. What insights do you gain about Jesus' victory, the nature of spiritual authority and your ministry?

3. In what ways can you learn about spiritual authority using Wesley's four pronged principles—learning from Scripture, history, reason and experience?

4. In what ways are you applying spiritual authority in your ministry?

5. What teaching or training have you done about spiritual authority with your ministry teams?

6. How can you activate and increase spiritual authority in your ministry?

7. How big is your God?

Our Mission Field—They're Waiting

Not only do we need to have God's viewpoint as we are sent on His mission with His authority, we also need to have an energizing perspective about our mission field. Scripture helps us "see" the reality of eternity in ways that haunt us and motivate us to action. In the light of eternity and the certainty of Christ's return, we are motivated with holy urgency!

"Summer is over, the harvest is past...and we are not saved." (Jeremiah 8:20 NIV)

"Multitudes, multitudes in the valley of decision! For the day of the Lord is near in the valley of decision." (Joel 3:14 NIV)

"But the exact day and hour? No one knows that, not even heaven's angels, not even the Son. Only the Father. So keep a sharp lookout, for you don't know the timetable. It's like a man who takes a trip, leaving home and putting his servants in

charge, each assigned a task and commanding the gatekeeper to stand watch. So, stay at your post, watching. You have no idea when the homeowner is returning, whether evening, midnight, cockcrow, or morning. You don't want him showing up unannounced, with you asleep on the job. I say it to you and I'm saying it to all: Stay at your post. Keep watch." (Mark 13:32-37 MSG)

Every Twenty Four Hours...

Think about what happens every day where you live...decisions are made that determine destinies!

Tom Clegg (*Missing in America*) and Dave Olson (*The American Church in Crisis*) have captured some statistics that make us look at the mission field in North America in some unsettling ways. Based on their findings, here's a picture of what will happen in the next twenty-four hours across North America:

- *11,350 babies will be born and 6,663 people will die*
- *6,110 couples will get married and there will be 3,110 divorces*
- *3,242 children will be aborted and there will be 4,106 illegitimate births*
- *87 will die by suicide, 36 will die from AIDS, 49 people will be murdered and there will be 43 alcohol related deaths*
- *12,267 children under 13 will take their first drink,*
- *2,948 children under 13 will have sex for the first time*
- *1,312 drop-outs, 4,400 teens will start smoking*
- *28,206 arrests, 4,274 of them drug related*
- *3,396 people will file bankruptcies, 63,288 will go on food stamps*
- *68,493 people will be treated for depression*
- *411 will convert to Islam*
- *827 will become Mormons*
- *16 churches will close their doors permanently*

Thousands will die without knowing the love of Christ...in a "Valley of Decision" called North America. Consider these facts about our North American mission field:

Fact #1: North America is the only continent where Christianity is <u>not</u> growing.

Fact #2: The decline in Christianity has been going on for nearly fifty years...there are now over 280 *million* unchurched people in the United States and Canada.

Fact #3: In the past 15 years churches in the USA have spent 500 *billion* dollars on buildings and programs...with *no* appreciable growth.

Fact #4: "The 80-80-80-80 Principle" On any given Sunday, about 80% of people are not attending any place of worship... 80% of churches are plateaued or in decline...yet 80% of unchurched people express interest and willingness to attend church if someone they knew and trusted would invite them...and 80% of Christians never invite anyone to church with them!

Fact #5: Over half of all churches in America did not add *one* new member through conversion last year.

Fact #6: About 20 churches per day are closing their doors. New churches are 11 times more effective reaching people for Christ than existing churches! We need nearly 5,000 more churches per year more than we are planting now just to keep up with population growth in the United States.

Fact #7: North America is the largest English speaking mission field in the world.

Fact #8: Far too many churched people believe and behave identically to their unchurched counterparts.

Fact #9: Conversions to other religions and dropouts from Christianity are escalating. It is estimated that 53,000 people leave churches every week and never come back. (*Exit Interviews,* George Hendricks)

Fact #10: No matter how you do the math, current conversion rates still point to one horrible conclusion: *lost people lose.*

If you don't live in North America, what are the *"Every Twenty Four Hours..."* realities of your mission field?

People are Waiting for Us to Come

When you see statistics like these, it can appear that our mission field is resistant. However, when we take a deeper look, we find that people are much more ready and receptive than we think. Thom Rainer, in his book *The Unchurched Next Door* offers general insights into the attitudes of unchurched people that are often different than we think. Here's a quick summary of some of Rainer's discoveries:

Our mission field is ripe...ready...and more receptive than we realize! People are waiting for us to come to them.

1. Most unchurched people prefer to attend church on Sunday morning, if they attend.

2. Females are most likely to be either the most receptive or antagonistic toward the Gospel.

3. Most unchurched people feel guilty about not attending church.

4. *82% of unchurched people are at least "somewhat likely" to attend church if they are invited*. Yet, only 21% of active church attenders invite anyone to church in a given year... and only 2% of Christians invite an unchurched person to attend church with them!

5. Very few unchurched people have had someone share with them how to become a Christian...and Christians have not been very influential in their lives.

6. Most unchurched people have positive views of pastors and the church.

7. Some types of "cold calls" are effective, but many aren't. The Lord may nudge us to engage a person we know in a spiritual conversation, but the majority of the time we should build relationships with people as we share Jesus with them.

8. Unchurched people would like to develop a real and sincere relationship with a Christian.

9. The attitudes of unchurched people are not correlated to geography, ethnicity or gender.

10. Many unchurched people are far more concerned about the spiritual well-being of their kids than themselves.

People are much more receptive spiritually than we give them credit for. In many ways they are waiting for us to come to them, listen to them, care for them and share what Jesus has done for us and what He can do for them, too!

Several years ago, I made a "Top Ten List" of what lost people are looking for from Christians. I asked my unchurched friends who weren't Christians yet to read my list and give me their thoughts. Most of them nodded their heads in agreement and invited me to further conversation. See how my "Top Ten" fits in with your thinking:

What Lost People Are Looking for from Christians

10. I don't care how much you know until I know how much you care.

9. Accept me as I am...have compassion for me, don't just condemn me because my life's a mess.

8. Ask "permission" to tell me about God, don't just push Him on me.

7. Use words I can understand.

6. Have a sense of humor! I want Christianity that can be enjoyed, not endured.

5. Don't tell me about your church. Labels don't mean much to me, I'm looking for people who live like they really love God.

4. Don't just tell me about your faith, show me your faith by serving others in love.

3. Find out about my world before you expect me to be interested in yours.

2. Tell me how God can make a difference in my daily life, not just in church on Sunday. If I'm going to be a Christian, I want it to work in real life.

1. Make Jesus real to me. Show me simply how to know Him from His Word and chances are I'll want to know Him, too. After all, I really do want to go to Heaven.

Multitudes hang in the balance...what should our response be to this vast mission field at our door?

You have nothing to do but save souls; therefore spend and be spent in this work; and go always not only to those who desire you, but to those who need you most."
—*John Wesley*

COACH YOURSELF FORWARD

1. What verses in Scripture "haunt" and motivate you to reach lost people?

2. Why is it so hard to see your community and nation as a mission field?

3. What stood out to you in the "Every Twenty Four Hours..." section?

4. Personalize the statistics we looked at. Who do you know that represents some of those stats? What are their names? What happens when "numbers become names"?

5. How did Thom Rainer's discoveries about the attitudes of unchurched people affect you?

6. How could you begin to apply what you learned from Rainer's study in your relationships?

7. Summarize what you've learned about joining Jesus on His redemptive mission in the mission field in your area.

FURTHER RESOURCES

The Unchurched Next Door, Thom Rainer. Zondervan, 2008.

Surprising Insights from the Previously Unchurched, Thom Rainer. Zondervan, 2008.

Lost in America, Tom Clegg. Group Publishing, 2001.

Missing in America, Tom Clegg. Group Publishing, 2007.

The American Church in Crisis, David Olson. Zondervan, 2008.

Nothing to Do But Save Souls, Robert Coleman. Francis Asbury Press, 2006.

Operation World, Jason Mandryk. InterVarsity Press, 2010.

"Shifting"
to Align with the Father's Purposes

The smell of fresh coffee filled the air as Tom and Bill placed their orders at the local coffee shop.

"I've been looking forward to this visit," said Tom. "I've been sharing with some fellow pastors around town and some of my ministry buddies around the country and in other countries what the Lord's been doing in me. Troy is planting a church in the heart of the city in a large urban setting. Chris pastors a church in a rural area where the church has been established a long time. Both the population of the area and the church are struggling with decline. Sue's on staff at a large suburban church. José is a missionary in another country. We are all in very different ministry environments, but we keep up with each other regularly. The interesting thing for me is that the Lord has been talking to them about the same issues! It's like the Holy Spirit has us on the same learning journey together."

Bill smiled, "It's interesting how the Spirit does that, isn't it? I've learned that when He's saying the same thing to different people in different places, I'd better pay close attention. Sounds like He's up to something that's bigger than just you and me."

Tom nodded in agreement. "I think you're right. Since we've been meeting, some things are really becoming clear for me. At the same time, it seems like I've got more questions than ever. My sense of call and mission are sharper than they've been for a long time. I feel like I'm closer to the Lord and seeing my world through His eyes in fresh ways. What I've been learning about my identity in Christ and spiritual authority has been really powerful. But if I'm going to live out His call, I can tell that I'm going to have to shift some things both in what I think and what I do. I've also got to help our church do so, too. How can I be so clear and so confused at the same time?"

Bill nodded. "I can relate. The Lord led me through a very similar process. Once He gripped me with His heart for lost people, He had to help me get aligned with His purposes. I had a lot of things that needed realignment! It started while I was still in ministry here in North America, but really became obvious when

I became a missionary to another culture. As the Lord helped me make some important shifts, it really helped me overcome the barriers I mentioned to you. I had focused primarily on a particular model of doing church as a typical church leader instead of making it first about Jesus and the people He'd sent me to reach."

First, I had to make intentional shifts to think, pray and act like a missionary. Before I asked anyone else do that, I had to be willing to do it myself. That may sound funny, but I found that there was a great difference between approaching life and ministry as missionary instead of a traditional pastor.

Bill paused and smiled at Tom, "What does that look like for you?"

Tom paused thoughtfully. "Honestly, I've been a traditional pastor. That's what I was trained to do. 'Pastor' is my title. That's where my gifts are. That's what my people expect of me.

Tom paused as if coming to a conclusion and a confession. "That's also been my excuse for not living like a missionary. I'm coming to realize that no matter what my ministry title, no matter where I am, no matter what my gifts and skills may be, I'm still called to live and bring the Good News of Jesus to everyone everywhere. In other words, God made me who I am on purpose...and I can be His missionary because of the way He made me."

"That's a powerful insight, Tom," Bill nodded. Now that you own that, in what ways are you becoming a missionary? How could you leverage your life more intentionally and redemptively? And...in what ways are you equipping your people to become great missionaries everywhere they go, too?"

Tom let out a long, slow breath. He was quiet for a moment. "Wow...it's hard enough to think about how to live more like a missionary myself. Realizing that I need to equip my people to become missionaries is a bit overwhelming right now."

Bill smiled with understanding. "Been there...I can relate. The principle I learned from Stephen Covey, "Begin with the end in mind," was important to me. Still, I had a lot of shifts to make so I could be more aligned with Him."

"What were the shifts the Lord helped you make?" Tom asked.

"There were many overall, but the more I've thought about it, things really boiled down to some very simple issues I had to put in right priority. That's when I felt like I was beginning to get aligned with the Father's purposes." I heard three words from Alan Hirsh that helped clarify and simplify some essential issues for me. Bill pulled out his notepad and wrote three words from left to right—

Christology...Missiology... Ecclesiology

"I had these essential issues out of order."

"How so?" Tom asked curiously.

"Good question. Basically, I had things backwards. I had started by determining what kind of church I wanted. I thought I was supposed to come up with a vision, start my ministry and then get people to come to my church. I hate to admit it, but I was really more in love with my vision and the kind of church I wanted than the Lord of the Church! On top of that, I realize now that I'd given little thought to whether the kind of church I wanted was what the people in my mission field needed. It didn't take me long to realize that my "ideal" church and the kind of church my mission field needed were not very compatible. My lifestyle was not very missional, much less my ministry. Some of the very things I was most enamored with about how I wanted to do church were actually hindering people from coming to Christ! It was a painful lesson to learn."

"What did you do?" Tom asked.

Bill smiled ruefully, "I wish I could tell you that I easily and willingly made the adjustments when I realized my priorities were messed up. After all, it was *my* vision for *my* church! I'm grateful for how patient and merciful Jesus was with me. He had to bring me to a fresh place of surrender...I had to lay down my vision and remember that it was *His* Church. Even more, it was all about *Him* and His Kingdom." Bill pointed to the words on the paper, "I had 'Ecclesiology'—my ministry and my idea of church—first. After giving my ministry and church back to Jesus, He now became first." He pointed to the word "Christology" on the paper. "Praying 'Thy Kingdom come...Thy will be done...' now had new meaning to me."

Tom paused for a moment, taking a long drink of coffee. "I

think you've been reading my mail. What you're describing hits close to home. There's another dimension to what you're describing, though. Not only am I dealing with my preference of what church should be like, there are the expectations and preferences of my people. Everyone has their own idea of what church should be according to their wants."

Bill chuckled. "Some things are universal, aren't they? That's where the Lord pointed out to me one more defining issue that had to be in proper alignment." He pointed to the world "Missiology" on the paper. "I now had Jesus as my top

> **The style of church is shaped by its mission field...the church must be more concerned about reaching the lost than losing the reached.**

priority, but I still had to discern what kind of church He wanted me to lead. That's where learning how to think and act as a missionary became so important. In order to know what kind of church the Lord wanted, not only did I need to understand how He'd wired and gifted me to lead, I also had to learn the needs of the people He'd called me to reach. I knew there were some Biblical essentials every church needs. I call them my 'Five E's for Every Church"-- but we had to adapt those essentials to connect to the culture we ministered in. The style of church is shaped by the mission field. Someone once told me that the church must be more concerned about reaching the lost than losing the reached. When I came to the place where I determined that my church had been designed around the priority of reaching lost people, things came into alignment for me... Christology, missiology, ecclesiology. Three simple words in the right priority made all the difference for me."

Tom nodded thoughtfully. "I get it...that makes real sense to me. I want to talk more about that, but you've made me curious. What are your 'Five E's for Every Church?"

Bill pulled out another sheet of paper and began to write. "These are just my way of describing what so many others have written about...but now the issue for me is *how* we would shape these essentials according to the needs and opportunities of our mission field." Bill finished writing and turned the paper around so Tom could read it. On it he had written:

<u>Five E's for Every Church</u>

Exalt God through worship
Edify people to wholeness
Equip people for the work of ministry
Evangelize through our witness
Extend His Kingdom to our world

Tom nodded as he read, "Those are pretty common thoughts alright. What isn't common is putting missiology as a key influence for ecclesiology. Your three words in that priority raise a lot more questions for me about the different shifts I'll need to make in my own thinking...and in our church's ministries. Could we make that our focus for the rest of the conversation? I'm enjoying the way you are coaching me."

"Sure," Bill said. "You set the agenda and we'll get you to some action steps. As a coach, I have a game plan to help you... and if I do it well, you'll leave with your own game plan you've discovered and developed yourself."

"Do you mind sharing with me what your coaching game plan is?" Tom asked. He smiled playfully. "Or is it a secret for only a select few?"

Bill returned Tom's tease with a grin. "No secrets, no code words, no special handshake. In fact, my game plan is pretty simple. As a coach, my goal is to see people grow to be more like Jesus and join Him on His redemptive mission...follow the Great Commandment and fulfill the Great Commission. Coaches help people grow by asking good questions that lead to discovery. That's better than just me giving advice. My coaching game plan is based on that word 'grow.'" Taking another sheet of paper, he wrote the word "GROW" vertically. "First, I always take time to listen, care and celebrate with the leader I'm coaching. We're paying attention to where God is working. Then we focus on a goal that leads us to action steps. Here's the path...

Listen, Care, Celebrate...G*R*O*W

    G is our <u>Goal</u>. That's our focus and determines the result you want to get from our conversation.

    R is for <u>Reality</u>. We paint a picture of what is really going on that is influencing our situation.

O is for <u>Options</u>. We ask the Holy Spirit to help us generate possibilities to accomplish our goal.

W is for <u>Will</u>...as in what "will" you do. This is where we clarify your action steps so you can move forward with your game plan."

Tom's eyes lit up with discovery. "I can see how you've been doing that with me. It sure helps. So...I've identified the goal... let's keep going."

Bill smiled. "Sounds good...glad we're at a place that gives us free refills on our coffee! This is going to be a fun conversation."

Coffee drinking, questions, animated conversation and discovery continued. When they were finished, Tom had written a list of biblical passages he wanted to study for further insights about God's missional priorities. Tom and Bill brainstormed a number of "shifts" that needed to be made for him to become a missional leader in a changing culture. Tom determined some ways he could leverage his life more intentionally and redemptively. They also made a list of different people in Tom's church that he would begin to converse with about what the Lord was doing in his heart.

Tom leaned back in his chair with the look of someone enjoying a job well done. "Thanks, Bill," Tom said. "You did a good job with your game plan as a coach...now I have a game plan to work on in the coming days. When can we get together again? Let's put something on the calendar now."

Bill pulled out his smart phone. "I'll be on the road for the next few weeks visiting other churches...how does the 25th look for you?"

Tom confirmed the date and time. "Got it...and next time I'm buying the coffee."

Form Missional Priorities

Although ministry can appear very complex, at the heart of things are some clear issues that need to be aligned with our Father's purposes. As my friend Dave DeVries, a veteran missionary, coach and church planting trainer observes, *"It's about alignment, not assignment; disciples, not decisions and being church more than doing church."* Let's revisit the essential issues Bill identified that formed his missional priorities. As you develop your ministry strategy, keep this "supernatural sequence" of priorities in mind:

Christology. It's always about Jesus and His Kingdom first and foremost...not about us, our church, affiliation or style. Start by focusing on Who sends us. We are chosen by, committed to and commissioned with authority by Jesus. Leighton Ford describes it as being "led more *by* Jesus so we can lead more *like* Jesus so we can lead more *to* Jesus."

Missiology. We join Jesus on His redemptive mission by discerning and developing a profile of our mission field. We want to fit and flourish where God has sent us so we can relate effectively and redemptively to people there. Key missional questions we need to ask include: Who has Jesus sent us to reach? What are their needs? How can we translate the Good News so they can understand, respond and become disciples of Jesus?

Ecclesiology. We discern and develop the form of "Church" needed to bring Christ to our mission field! A key missional question is, "What *could* church look like to bring Jesus to this culture?"

The missional process can be described in several other ways:

- "Sent...Student...Servant...Storyteller."

- "Discerning listening, divine appointments, determining needs, developing ministries, deploying teams..."

- "Leaving our own, living among, listening to, loving redemptively, linking to community."

Scriptural Insights for Missional Ministry

The principles of Scripture give us the keys to developing the unique missional game plan for your mission field. Although the principles are woven throughout the whole Bible, there are some places that are especially helpful for us to gain insights for missional ministry. Let's highlight a few passages briefly. For a fuller outline of these passages see Appendix B.

Joshua: God's Field Guide to Take the Promised Land

The Book of Joshua is still used by military leaders as a great field manual. It is also a powerful guide for spiritual warriors today. Throughout Joshua you'll find how God sanctified and shaped His leaders, gave them strategies for engaging their adversaries and supernaturally brought victory.

Numbers 13: Spy Out the Land

As you seek God's wisdom for your ministry, remember these key lessons from Numbers 13:

1. Like Moses did with the 12 spies, it is important to "spy out the land" before you go in. This is called spiritual surveying or mapping.
2. Like the 12 spies, you need to be able to identify the strongholds of the enemy that keep people captive.
3. Like Joshua and Caleb, you must also identify the opportunities and assets of the land and "redemptive gifts" Jesus wants to release to set people free.
4. Remember, God is greater than the enemy! It's His power and authority that makes the difference!

Acts: God's Multiplication Manual

Apostles and disciples in the early Church were the first to live out Great Commission strategies with the supernatural anointing and authority of the Holy Spirit. The combination of sanctified love from a pure heart, spiritual authority to defeat Satan and supernatural power for miracles made biblical multiplication an amazing reality. Disciples today still look to Acts for the principles that make multiplication possible.

Luke 9 and 10: Jesus' Strategy for Reaching New Communities

Luke 9 and 10 describe how Jesus commissioned His team and sent them ahead of Him to prepare the way for His arrival. The integration of spiritual authority with gracious incarnational and invitational ministry we find in Luke is the basis for missional ministry strategy today.

Making Missional Shifts

"Missional" means we approach ministry as missionaries...sent by God and blessed by Him to be a blessing to others! Our commission is as old as God's covenant with Abraham in Genesis 12. In our generation it becomes the personal expression of the Great Commandment of Matthew 22:36-40 and the Great Commission of Matthew 28:18-20.

Reggie McNeal, in his book *Missional Renaissance,* suggests three major shifts we must make:
1. From inward to outward—focusing on the lost more than the already converted.
2. From doing programs to developing people—focusing on equipping disciples to be disciple-makers.
3. From Church to Kingdom—focusing on the big picture of what God is doing, not just our specific church.

In other words, we need to learn to distinguish between missional and attractional approaches to ministry. The idea of becoming more missional is resonating with many leaders. The majority of existing churches have had more of an attractional approach. They consciously or unconsciously expect people to come to them so they can tell them about Jesus. "Outreach" is usually tied to events or programs to get people to come to a building. When people do come, though, attractional churches must figure out how to translate God's Good News so it is understandable for unchurched people. More and more people in our culture don't know God and aren't familiar with church language and practices. As Colossians 4:2-6 reminds us, it is our responsibility and privilege to take the mystery out of knowing God. It is our responsibility to translate the Good News so others can understand. Missional leaders realize that it should not be the unchurched person's burden to have to interpret what we are saying. Missional and attractional approaches ministry are both important...not "either/or" but "both/and."

This "both/and" perspective requires that we make some shifts in our ministry philosophy and practice. Let's look at some shifts that are affecting ministry in many cultures:

Generational:	Builder/Boomer	to	Buster/Millennial
Cultural:	Modern	to	Postmodern & Pre-modern
Philosophical:	Organizational	to	Organic/relational
Method:	Attractional	to	Missional/"Missionally Attractive"

Supported:	Fully funded	to	Bi-vocational
Organizational:	Denomination/ District centered	to	Parent/Multi-site
Scope:	Local	to	"Glocal"
Planting Strategy:	Attract a crowd, start a church	to	Engage community... do ministry...be church... launch services
Posture:	Apologist	to	Missiologist
	Proclamational	to	Incarnational/Invitational
	Head first/word	to	Heart first/worship/ experience
Training:	Content/information centered	to	Context/application centered and coached

There's been lots of discussion about the words "attractional" and "missional" in recent years. We need to do both...but be missional first! When we go (missional), we earn the right to be heard. We build bridges for people to come to our gatherings...in homes, coffee shops and church buildings. When people come to us, (attractional), we must work hard to translate timeless truth in timely ways...to take the mystery out of knowing Christ. Simply put, our game plan has to be intentionally *incarnational* and *invitational*...not only demonstrating God's love in practical ways, but also intentionally inviting people to make the decision to become a disciple of Jesus.

Shifts We Must Make as Missional Leaders

From...	*To...*
Going to church	Being the Church
Missionaries are ministry specialists	My special ministry is to be a missionary!
"Losing" people from our church	Sending people on God's mission
Giving up our resources	Investing God's provisions
We're too weak	We have authority through Jesus

From...	To...
We can't afford this	We can't afford not to!
One bigger church	More churches reaching more people
Church is for Christians	Ministry for pre-Christians
Ministry for me	I'm a minister for others
Splitting/dividing	Multiplying/expanding
Programs/preferences	Mission-focused ministries meeting needs
My church first	Jesus' mission as our primary passion
Escape or entertain culture	Engage culture
"Come in here"	"Go out there"
"Come...listen to me"	"Go...listen to you...serve"
Head first	Heart first
Program/institutional	Personal/relational
Start churches/do ministry	Do ministry/start churches
Proclamational	Incarnational and invitational
Believer-focused	Harvest-focused
Church-centered	Community-based
Wesley's theology	Wesley's theology *and* methods
"Believe...then you can belong"	"Belong...and you'll want to believe"

Understanding and Leading Change

Different studies have shown similar insights about how people tend to feel toward change:

2-3% are "innovators" who create new ideas and initiate change.

13-14% are "early adopters" who don't generate ideas but love to try them out. Once these two groups of people are engaged and committed, it often becomes the "tipping point" for the new ideas to take hold in the rest of the group or culture.

34% are "early majority" who like to bring the idea into the mainstream.

34% are "late majority" who will try an idea when they feel it's safe and acceptable.

16% are "laggards" who resist change. A few will never accept it.

Recognizing those different attitudes toward change and the "timing" of how people accept and implement change is a vital aspect of leadership. A helpful resource about leading people through the change process is *Unfreezing Moves: Following Jesus into the Mission Field* by Bill Easum. The heart of his book can be summed up by sharing your heart about going on mission with Jesus, finding people who also want missional change, form them into a team, communicate to the rest of the church that they are "field testing" some new ideas and allow the stories of their experiences to influence others. As more people see the benefits of the new ideas, they will want to experience them, too. Change comes wisely, progressively and intentionally.

My friend and former Church Resource Ministries (CRM) teammate Phil Newell offers this wise insight:

> "The 5,000 pound elephant in the room is Bill's church. How is he leading the church into missional insight and movement? Unity is developed around Biblical values rather than starting with a leader's vision. Values (the heart level essential issues which determine our priorities, influence our decisions and determine where we will invest our time and money) represent the true culture of a church. Values are a reality that will trump any attempt to add or adjust 'vision.' Until values are identified, addressed and reframed biblically, not much tends to happen missionally. It takes time for that to happen."

One of the best ways to communicate values is through stories. As Bill shared his own story of God's work in his life and the stories of the people in their mission field, it touches people on a heart level. That's where values change. Making true missional shifts always begin in the heart.

Leverage Your Life

Many Christians and Christian leaders agree with the need to be more intentional and missional, but struggle with having time to do so. Another huge shift for us to make is: finding time for God and being missional in my schedule and humbly letting the Spirit fit me into *His* schedule...leveraging my life more intentionally and redemptively!

Here are some ways you can think about leveraging your life:

"Leverage Your Life"
Discovering Ways to Make a Difference for God in Your Daily Life
2 Corinthians 5:14-21

Pay Attention...Discern Where God is at Work

1. What do you *enjoy* that could be leveraged redemptively? What energizes you? Interests, hobbies, skills...

2. What *experiences* have you had that the Lord could leverage redemptively?

3. What existing *environments* could you leverage more intentionally for redemptive relationships?
   - Work
   - Friendships/relationships
   - Kids' activities (if it applies)
   - Neighbors
   - Other activities

4. What "divine *encouragements*" do you sense from the Lord to be used by Him...both inside and outside the church?
   - What burdens you?
   - What are you passionate about?
   - What desires do you have to be used by the Lord?
   - What sense of calling do you have?
   - What doors of opportunity do you see?

Practical Application...Deploy Daily as God's Missionary!

1. As you prayed through how you can leverage your life... through what you enjoy, experiences you've had, environments you live in and divine encouragements from the Lord,

what has the Lord called to your attention?

2. How can you be more specific and intentional where the Lord is leading you? Who...where...when...how? Develop at least two specific and doable action steps you can implement in the next two weeks.

3. Who can you have join you in prayer? Who can check in with you for healthy accountability as you leverage your life as God's missionary?

Discerning Your Ministry Contribution

Key verses: Psalm 32:8; Romans 12:1-3; Philippians 2:13
Key question: *"When do I most often experience God's power, joy and fruit in my life?"*

1. The people and circumstances that have most shaped my life are_____.

2. The qualities of character I most want God to shape into my own life are _____
_____. Why?

3. People who know me well believe I am most used by God when I am involved in _____
_____. Why?

4. My daily activities that contribute most to God's kingdom are
_____
_____. Why?

5. When I think about making a difference for God, I would love to focus more on_____
_____. Why?

6. Though I may have dismissed the thought many times for various reasons, I sometimes feel I really should be doing_____
_____. Why?

7. When people talk about a passion for ministry, I often begin to think about giving my life to accomplishing_____
_____. Why?

Personal vision calls for discerning the influences that have created a passion for God and a passion to accomplish something special for His Kingdom. What insights or themes surfaced in my reflections?

COACH YOURSELF FORWARD

1. When you look at the words "Christology, Missiology, Ecclesiology," what order would best describe your current personal priorities?

2. What order would best describe your church's current actual priorities?

3. What issues need to be addressed in order to have your life and ministry aligned with God's missional priorities?

4. What insights did you gain from the different biblical passages we highlighted? (See Appendix B)

5. How can you begin to apply those insights to your present ministry?

6. What shifts do you need to make in order to be more intentionally missional? What are your next steps to make those shifts?

7. As you processed the "Leveraging Your Life" section, what are your action steps?

Resistance

When Tom and Bill got together again a few weeks later, Bill noticed that Tom was more somber than usual.

"I've been out raising support and haven't been around for about a month," Bill said. "What's been happening since we were together last?"

Tom stirred his coffee for a moment before replying. "I wish I could tell you that everything's been good, but I've run into some unexpected and difficult things lately."

Bill leaned forward, listening intently. "What's been happening?"

Tom shook his head slightly as he looked up at Bill. "You know how excited I've been about the Lord giving me fresh passion for reaching lost people. I want it to become our defining priority of my life and for our church so everything we do will align to His Great Commission. I've begun sharing with others what the Lord's been doing in my own heart. I've been sharing with some of our key leaders at church and inviting them to pray with me about how our church could become more intentional about reaching our community. I want to be wise about how I lead our church in light of the shifts we'll need to make in our priorities and ministries."

Bill nodded, "That sounds good, Tom. How have people been responding?"

"That's what's been surprising and somewhat discouraging to me. I thought everyone would be excited with me about joining Jesus on His redemptive mission. Some have been. They told me that this is just what they've been praying about for us as a church. That's been really encouraging. The Holy Spirit has been talking to others about the same things He's been impressing on my heart!" Then Tom shook his head again. "Others...well, the response I've gotten from others wasn't what I expected. Some of my leaders have been doubtful and some actually resistant to reaching lost people. They've been coming up with reasons that just don't make sense."

"I understand," said Bill. "When our family became missionaries, a wise older missionary said to us, 'You'll be surprised at who supports you and surprised at who doesn't.' They were right, both financially and practically. Some people struggle with change in general. It takes wise leadership to help people move through stages of change to follow the Lord into His harvest fields. For others, however, it reveals their true priorities. It's like the principle that Jesus taught in His parable about the tenants in Mark 12...harvest time reveals the heart."

Tom nodded. "I know people process change in different ways. Leading my people through this kind of change will *"Harvest time reveals the heart."* really stretch me as a leader. It won't be easy, but I'm willing to do whatever it takes. However, there has been some other things happening—more than just people's resistance to going beyond what is familiar and comfortable. Things have been happening that are not normal. Some of my leaders tell me that they've been dealing with unusual stresses in their marriage. I've been experiencing more temptation than I have in a long time. One of my kids has suddenly gotten sick and we don't know why. Also, it seems like there's more tension and conflict among people at church lately. It seems like we're under attack or something."

"You are under attack," Bill responded. "Not all resistance to change is a spiritual attack as we learned when we talked about how people respond to change. However, we have to understand the reality of spiritual warfare. We went through many similar things on our ministry team. When you become intentional about reaching lost people, you become a special target for Satan. We had a lot to learn about spiritual warfare and the power of prayer. That's why I said that understanding spiritual authority was so important. If the enemy can deter us from pursuing Christ's mission, he's won. When the spiritual resistance is strongest, you're closest to seeing God really break through."

Tom smiled ruefully, "We must be close to a breakthrough, then, because the resistance has been really fierce. I really do have a lot to learn about how to deal with that kind of spiritual attack. The devil doesn't fight fair. When he goes after my family and my people like that, I've got to do something about it."

"You don't have to do it alone, Tom. The Lord's got a lot of people He's summoning to be on your team to pray you through this. I'm glad to be on your team!" Bill looked at Tom earnestly, "How are you keeping your intercessors informed and active about these issues?"

"How are you keeping your intercessors informed and active?"

For a long moment Tom was silent, with a look of troubled realization on his face. "Oh...I've forgotten about that! I haven't even developed a prayer team to pray for me, my family and our ministry! I've left us unprotected. That's got to change."

Bill nodded in agreement, "That's a great insight, Tom. I had to come to the same realization. Prayer that releases the power of God wins the battle. We win first in the unseen realm before we see victory in the visible realm. It sounds like you need to develop a prayer team and a prayer strategy for you and your church."

"That's exactly what I need," Tom replied. "Could we focus our coaching on those issues today?"

"Sounds good," Bill said. "Let's come up with a game plan for prayer."

Together Tom and Bill identified some options for a prayer team and intercession strategies. Occasionally Bill would share an insight or a story from his own experience, but each time he quickly brought things back to Tom's situation, asking questions that allowed Tom to apply those insights personally. When they were finished, Tom had several action steps for recruiting his own prayer team and keeping them informed and active. He also adapted some prayer strategies Bill had used on his mission field and asked Bill if he would help train people at church how to begin praying intentionally for their families, neighbors, work places and community. This time they both captured their thoughts in notebooks they'd begun using for their coaching appointments.

Bill smiled at Tom as he watched him writing down his game plan. As Tom identified each goal, Bill continued to ask him questions to further clarify his action steps.

"Thanks, Bill. I really appreciate how you help me take my ideas and turn them into something I can actually do. When you talk about leaving with a game plan that I've created and own, I understand it more and more."

"Good work, Tom," Bill said. "What we just did at the end was to turn your objectives into "S*M*A*R*T" action steps." He wrote the acronym "S*M*A*R*T" on a piece of paper. Here's what we did...we made each action step...

Specific
Measureable
Attainable
Relevant
Time bound

"The difference between having some good ideas and really developing clear action steps is developing your own SMART game plan to move forward."

Tom smiled back, "Thanks for letting me know what you are doing and why you are doing it as you coach me. Do you mind if I use what I'm learning from you with my leaders?"

Bill nodded his agreement, "I was hoping you'd say that. One of the greatest joys for me as a coach is when I see leaders like you begin to coach others, too. If it's all right with you, I'd like to not only coach you, but also start equipping you to coach others."

"If I can help my leaders like you're helping me, then it's more than all right. We need this...keep it up!"

Activate Strategic Intercession

Let's focus on the priority of intentional intercession. Prayer is not just a program. It is the lifestyle and lifeblood of missional leaders and missional churches. Although it's been often said that everything rises and falls on leadership, it is vital to affirm that leaders rise or fall on prayer.

Intentional missional ministry relies on strategic intercession as its indispensable power source. If you want to love like you've never loved before, lead like you've never led before, care like you've never cared before, share like you've never shared before, go where you've never gone before...then pray like you've never prayed before!

Developing Your Spheres of Intercessors

Developing a prayer team that protects spiritual leaders is often dramatically undervalued. A good model to follow is Jesus' 3-12-70/120 expanding spheres of people. What could your teams of intercessors look like?

- **Your "Inner Circle"**—those who know you best, have the gift of intercession and are called to pray for you. You can tell them everything...your deepest needs and issues. The Inner Circle is typically three to five people. Communicate with them often...and consider them always "on call" for prayer no matter what time of day or night. Who are those in your "Inner Circle"?

- **Your "Twelve"**—people who know you well and you trust to pray often for you. You can share with them almost everything...they will pray for you more than your projects. These people need to be informed regularly. Who are your "Twelve"?

- *Your "Extended Community"*—these are people who know you and will occasionally pray for you. They will be interested in general information and requests about your ministry. You will probably communicate with them every one to three months.

One of the essential priorities for leaders is to keep their intercessors informed, active and involved. What do you share with your prayer warriors? Here are three areas that inform intercessors:

1. *"News"*—what's happening in your family and ministry? Tell stories of the people you are reaching.
2. *"Numbers"*—share specifics about your results.
3. *"Needs"*—share your personal and ministry needs. If they don't know what you need, they can't pray for specific answers!

Praying for Others

Statistics do tell a story, but for us to truly be gripped by the urgency of the needs of our mission field, <u>numbers must become names</u>.

When a statistic becomes a face we can see and a name that we know...

When we see people as lost and truly in danger in the here and now and in the hereafter...

When the love of Jesus compels us to go regardless of the cost...

When our mission is that simple and clear...

Then everything we do as a church is defined and measured by joining Jesus on His redemptive mission in our world *and we pray accordingly.*

If you want to increase the harvest, you've got to intensify your intercession!

A useful model to intensify your intercession is to develop a "My Most Wanted" prayer list. These are the people Jesus has given me a burden to pray for, listen to, serve willingly and share graciously with so they might come to know Him, too.

"My Most Wanted" Intercession List
1.

2.

3.

4.

5.

6.

7.

8.

9.

10.

How To "B*L*E*S*S" Others in Prayer

When we pray for God's Kingdom to come, we are asking the Lord to work in people's lives in such a way that they recognize His powerful love drawing them to know Him. As you take time to get to know people and listen for their needs, the Lord will give you wisdom and authority to pray for them. A prayer strategy I've learned from Ed Silvoso gives a simple guideline to pray specifically and consistently for these key needs in people's lives. He calls it being a "lighthouse of prayer." We approach our prayer for others from a posture of blessing them with what God wants for them. As Scripture reminds us in Romans 2:4, the Lord's kindness leads us to repentance. As people see God at work in their lives, they are more open to Him. Ask the Lord to "bless" people in the following ways:

Body—their physical needs (health issues, freedom from addictions, etc.)

Labor—their work (workplace relationships, employment needs)

Emotions—their "felt" needs for love, peace, faith, hope

Social—their relationships with family, friends, neighbors and coworkers

Spiritual—God's best for their lives—His forgiveness, peace, power and a home in Heaven

You can "prayer walk (or drive)" your neighborhood, school, place of work. Pray with His discernment and authority. Ask the Lord of the Harvest for the number of people He wants you to influence for His Kingdom...ask Him for the faith to do it! God is with you as you pray! Seek to develop a lifestyle of prayer...you will be amazed at the answers to prayer God will bring...miracles are waiting!

COACH YOURSELF FORWARD

1. How are you developing your intercessory team?

2. How will you help other leaders in your ministry develop their prayer teams?

3. Who's on your "Most Wanted" personal intercession list? Who else might the Lord want you to add?

4. How will you help your people identify and begin to intercede intentionally for the people God burdens them to pray for?

5. In what ways can you increase the prayer temperature and involvement in your ministry?

6. In what ways can you be intentional about equipping your people to become intercessors in their neighborhoods, schools and work places?

7. What "S*M*A*R*T" goals can you develop as a game plan for your ministry of intercession?

FURTHER RESOURCES

Partners in Prayer, John Maxwell. Thomas Nelson, 1996.

Coaching Guideline by Tim Roehl (see Appendix A).

Missional Renaissance, Reggie McNeal. Jossey-Bass, 2009.

TransforMissional Coaching, Tim Roehl and Steve Ogne. B&H Publishing, 2008.

The Celtic Way of Evangelism, George Hunter. Abington Press, 2010.

And: The Church Gathered and Scattered, Hugh Halter and Matt Smay. Zondervan, 2010.

Six Word Lessons to Discover Missional Living, Dave DeVries. Leading on the Edge International, 2010.

That None Should Perish, Ed Silvoso and C. Peter Wagner, Chosen Books, 1995.

Prayer Evangelism, Ed Silvoso, Regal Books, 2000.

Seven Habits of Highly Effective People, Stephen R Covey, DC Books, 2005.

Unfreezing Moves: Following Jesus into the Mission Field, Bill Easum. Abingdon Press, 2002.

<u>Appendix B</u>
Scripture Studies

<u>Appendix C</u>
"Missional Shifts"
"Leverage Your Life"
"Spheres of Intercessors"

"Studying"
Your Mission Field Redemptively

When Tom and Bill got together again, they spent time celebrating the accomplishments they'd been working on. Tom shared how the Lord was growing his passion for lost people. "Every day the way I view my world is different now," Tom said. "I see people through the Father's eyes and feel His love for them. I long for them to know His forgiveness and freedom. I've been more sensitive and intentional about praying for, relating to and serving my neighbors. I can see the difference leveraging my life more intentionally and redemptively is making. It's been coming through in my conversations and my preaching. I have more confidence as I grow in my identity in Christ and understand spiritual authority. As I share what the Lord's doing in me, it's been exciting to see how He's been doing the same thing for others—people in my church, other pastors in our community and my ministry buddies around the world. Our leaders are catching the vision to make the Great Commission our priority. I can tell the difference now that I have a prayer team interceding for us. As we've begun to pray at church and around our community, opportunities are opening up to us like never before. So many good things have been happening, but I just know there's so much more to come!"

Bill smiled in agreement. "It's good for us to stop, pay attention and celebrate what the Lord's been doing. The journey is long. When we look at how much there is to do, it can be overwhelming. But when we stop and celebrate how far the Lord has brought us, it keeps us encouraged and fuels us to keep on moving ahead. How about if we spend some time just thanking Jesus for what we're celebrating here?"

Tom's response was to bow his head and pour out his heart in thanks and plead with the Lord to trust him and their church for more souls. Bill murmured his agreement and continued with a prayer that blended adoration and authority in a powerful way. The two men basked in the Presence and sensed the reality of what Psalm 92:10 calls being "anointed with fresh oil."

When Tom looked up again, his face was glowing. "Wow... there's nothing like meeting with Jesus like this! Thanks again for walking with me, Bill. And, thanks for the message you preached at our church Sunday. I sure appreciated how you helped us understand that we are all missionaries where God places us. The way you described the church as disciples making disciples making disciples was powerful. The stories you told about how you do that in your own life inspired us to believe God can use us like that, too. A lot of people talked to me about the way those concepts are reshaping their walk with Jesus and their daily lives. If we are to become missionaries to our own community, I wanted my people to hear your heart, as well as some of the strategies the Lord helped you develop. I'm realizing we have to be spiritual *and* strategic in our ministry. You're helping me pay attention to both."

Bill smiled his thanks. "I appreciate that, Tom. A key principle for me is, *"What you want your people to do corporately you have to model personally."* It's not uncommon for leaders to go to an extreme on either side. Some are so spiritual that they think they should just pray and the rest is up to God. That can be a recipe for inactivity. Others go to the other extreme and make it all about strategy and planning. It becomes all about numbers and our self-effort. I like the old saying that we're supposed to pray as if everything depends on God and work as if everything depends on us. I would observe that we have been mostly paying attention to the spiritual side of things so far in our coaching journey. The Lord has to do His work *in* us to prepare us for the work He wants to do *through* us."

"What you want your people to do corporately you have to model personally"

"He's sure been doing a lot in me," said Tom. "I'm hungry for the Lord to do more through me. I've been thinking about how to make the missional shifts we talked about and I've been praying more intentionally for my mission field. I really want to know more about the *missiology* part of our missional priorities. How can I become more intentional about discerning the needs of our mission field? In my ministry training I learned how to exegete Scriptures but I didn't learn much about how to exegete culture. I need to learn more about how to think and act like a missionary so we can bring Jesus to our community. How do we do that?"

Bill smiled. "I would agree that we are ready to drill down on that issue now. When I became a missionary, I had a burning desire to bring Christ to the people of our mission field. I thought all I needed to do was to start having services, invite them to come and do church like I was used to. It was all about getting them to listen to me." He chuckled. "I soon learned that I had things backward again. I needed to listen first. I knew I'd been sent, but I didn't know what I needed to help them come to Jesus. The power of God's call got me there and kept me there, but I still had a lot to learn."

"That's where I am," said Tom. "But you must have done something right when we look at all the fruit your ministry is bearing in a place most people feel is nearly unreachable. What did you do?"

Bill said, "I was desperate to figure out what to do. Thankfully, the Lord made sure that I met another missionary who became a mentor and a coach to me. That sure made a big difference."

Tom said, "I really appreciate what I'm learning about coaching. It's already making a difference in how I lead my people. What's the difference between a mentor and a coach?"

"Good question...and an important distinction," replied Bill. "The simplest way to describe the difference between the two ministries is this: a mentor pours in and a coach pulls out. When I tell you some of my story or share some ideas, that's more mentoring. When I ask the questions using our "listen, care, celebrate–GROW" pathway to help pull out your insights and develop your game plan...that's coaching."

Tom's eyes lit up with an "aha" of understanding. "That's really helpful. So, would you mind pouring in some of what you learned? I'm a sponge."

Bill laughed, "Sure. As my coach worked with me, I came up with four key words that helped me form a pathway to discern the needs and develop a game plan for our mission field." He pulled out a sheet of paper and wrote,

Sent...Student...Servant...Storyteller

"I feel like I understand the *sent* part now," said Tom. "What do the other words mean?"

"Well," Bill responded, "before I could tell God's story in a way that people could understand and relate to, I had to assume a listening, learning posture and become a student of the culture. My coach helped me identify the questions that I needed to ask and then learn about. That's the *student* part. As we discerned the needs and opportunities, we then asked the Lord in what ways He wanted us to address those needs and opportunities that fit who we were as a team. That became the *servant* part of our ministry pathway. As we demonstrated God's love in practical ways, He gave us relationship and favor with people. We listened to their stories and began to share ours. We earned the right to have spiritual conversations and invite people to our gatherings because we focused on *being* the church rather than *having* church. Then we were able to determine how to tell God's Good News in a way they could understand and respond to...we learned to translate the Gospel for them. We designed our church services and ministries based on how to best tell the story of Jesus for them. That's the *storyteller* part."

"Cool," said Tom, his head nodding in agreement. "It fits right in with your *Christology, Missiology, Ecclesiology* principles. This is the practical application of those missional priorities, right?"

"Right," said Bill. "The priorities are pretty simple and clear and the pathway is, too. What you learn and do as a student, servant and storyteller will help you develop a unique game plan for ministry to your mission field." Pointing to the words he asked, "Where are you right now on that pathway?"

Tom thought for a moment. "Like I said, we are getting a grasp on what it means to be sent. That's influencing all we do. It looks like my next focus personally and as a church needs to be on becoming students of our mission field. We don't know what we need to know yet to be and bring Good News to our community. You said you came up with some questions that helped you study your mission field redemptively. What were they?

"Tell you what," said Bill. "How about if we come up with your game plan for that right now? I'm sure the questions you think of will be very similar to mine."

Tom pulled out a sheet of paper. "I know where we're going," he smiled. "Let's do the GROW and drill down. You pour in some and then pull out of me what we need to do."

Together they worked through the coaching process and came up with a list of questions that would help Tom study their mission field redemptively. It included questions such as:

1. What are the needs in our mission field Jesus wants us to meet to bring people to know Him?
2. What are the positive qualities of the culture here that can become bridges for the Good News? What are the negative qualities of the culture here that are barriers we must overcome?
3. What are the spiritual strongholds holding people back in this area from knowing Jesus?
4. What redemptive gifts does the Lord want to release to this area to set people free?
5. Who knows what we need to know? Who are the "sphere of influence leaders" in this area who can give us perspective on the needs?
6. Who are the people of peace God wants us to meet?
7. Who are the intercessors and other spiritual leaders of this area we can join with in ministry?

Bill and Tom then developed several approaches Tom and his team could use to answer each question.

Tom looked up from the extensive notes he had captured. "I really like this. It makes me wonder why we haven't been doing these things before! He pointed to one approach they had developed. I'm especially excited about the 'Check the S*o*I*L' listening we'll be doing."

Bill said, "It's always gratifying to see how the Holy Spirit goes ahead of us. I'll be interested to know what you learn from your listening and where you find what I like to call 'receptive soil.' We're going to find that the Lord of the Harvest already has a game plan for your harvest fields. It will unfold itself as the Spirit leads us and that will become our strategy."

Tom smiled, "I believe that. As we study our mission field redemptively, let's pray that we'll learn what He wants us to know! Lead out, Bill, will you?"

Bill's response was to ask the Lord for His wisdom, favor and discernment for Tom and his team, thanking Him that He was already ahead of them preparing the way. Both men had a sense of anticipation that some wonderful conversations and discoveries were coming.

Gather Statistical Insights

Demographic statistics give us an overview of our mission field necessary for discerning the needs and opportunities around us. Websites such as www.easidemographics.com and www.perceptgroup.com are good starting places for people in North America. You can find similar ways of doing demographic research for other nations.

Research requires limiting the scope of your study. Through prayer, determine the size of your "parish" or "circle of accountability." In a densely populated area, your parish may be smaller geographically, but broader ethnically. You may feel led to focus especially on a particular segment of your parish. As you review demographic facts, pay attention to the issues that will help develop a profile of the needs of people in your area. Pastor Rick Warren of Saddleback Church took this kind of study to profile a typical resident of his community that he nicknamed "Saddleback Sam." Use statistical information to create a real picture of the people you are called to reach.

What do demographic statistics tell you about your mission field in the following areas?

Ethnic diversity—What are the different ethnic groups represented? Who is the majority group or groups? Who are the minority groups? How many languages are spoken? How has the population changed over the past ten years in terms of numbers and ethnicity? What are the projections for the next ten years?

Economic issues—What is the median income and income range in your area? How would your area be described in terms of income and lifestyles?

Employment—What are the different kinds of employment in the area? Who are the major employers? What is the mixture of "white collar," "blue collar" and "no collar" (information and technology) jobs in your area? What is the unemployment rate? How far do people drive to go to work?

Educational—What are the different schools in the area? What is the average level of education?

Entertainment—What kind of entertainment businesses are there? How many of them are harmful to healthy families and communities? Where and how do people spend their money? What kind of recreation facilities are in the area?

"Environment"—How will ministry in this area be affected by local geography, politics and social attitudes?

Family make up—How many are married? Single? What percentage of people fit into the different ages and stages of life (such as children, teens, young adults, senior citizens, etc.)? How many single parent families are there?

Churches—What kinds of churches or spiritual centers of other religions are in the area? What does that tell you?

As you further review the demographic information, what are other insights you should note? Ask the Holy Spirit to point out what He wants you to focus on.

After you review these initial demographic findings, what are your impressions about the kinds of churches and ministries needed for people in your area?

Survey Spiritual Dynamics

When we do spiritual survey work (some call this spiritual mapping or spiritual detective work), we are seeking to discern the spiritual dynamics and influences of our mission field. What we can't see statistically is manifested in the attitudes and actions of people. Some describe it this way: "What's happening in the supernatural is manifested in the natural." Our spiritual surveying further informs our intercession and helps form ministry strategies.

As you "map" your mission field, exegete the culture (which I simply define as "the way we do things around here") from two key perspectives:

First, what are the good qualities of this culture that we can use as bridges for the Good News? Second, what are the qualities of this culture corrupted by sin that represent barriers we must overcome?

Begin your spiritual survey work by doing prayer walks or prayer drives of your area. Just be out among people! As you walk or drive, record your observations or impressions. Ask the Lord to give you His perspective so you can "see" with His eyes and heart.

Another key part of doing spiritual survey work is to ask the Lord to lead you to spiritually discerning people in the area. These people are often doing the quiet, somewhat hidden work of intercession. Some have a long history in your area. Ask other spiritual leaders who the prayer warriors are they know. Some may be in your church, some may be in other churches. Many will be women. "Praying grannies" are well known in heaven! When you find them, listen closely to their wisdom and benefit from the power of their prayer lives.

Here are some important issues for seeking discernment while doing your spiritual survey work.

1. **Pray!** Ask God to give you discernment regarding the strongholds of the enemy, the needs of the people and the redemptive possibilities He has in mind.

2. Review the **past.** As you understand the history of your area, you can begin to discern the spiritual influences at work. What important events have taken place? Who were the pioneers of the area? What were their intentions and priorities for this area? What attitudes and behaviors have long been part of the culture?

3. Look at significant **places.** Pay attention to the houses, yards, decorations, signs, businesses and public spaces. How well do people take care of things? Look for monuments, the layout of the area, statues, spiritual places...anything that might help you identify spiritual influences and idols.

4. Look for the seats of **power.** Get to know the government, business, education and religion centers. Who are the key people in positions of power in the area? What are their attitudes toward the things of God?

5. Some communities are highly resistant to God's work. Others (sometimes close but in a different part of the same city or across a geographic boundary) are open and receptive to the Lord. Seek to discern the reasons for those attitudes.

6. What are the **practices** of the community? What are the main festivals or celebrations? What kind of activities do many people participate in? What brings people together? What divides them? Pay attention to sports and recreation leagues, community groups, niche groups, etc. These help us understand the values and priorities of the people in your mission field.

7. Learn about the spiritual **problems** you need to address. What kinds of influence are there from other religions, cults or occult groups? What holds people back from finding God? Find out what people believe in your area.

8. What people believe influences how they behave. Although people's theological beliefs are important, the best place to understand problems will be in the descriptions of more tangible issues around people's physical, material and emotional needs. *Learn to listen for people's longings...that's where we really hear them on their heart level...and find the keys to their hearts.* As you listen to people's longings, you'll better understand what they believe about the essential issues of Christian faith such as God, Jesus Christ, the Bible, Heaven, Hell, sin, salvation, church...and other particular religious practices, such as praying for or to the dead, idols, new age practices, etc.

> *"Learn to listen for people's longings...that's where we really hear them on their heart level... and find the keys to their hearts."*

9. Listen to, link with and pray with your Kingdom **partners**. What other churches are in the area? Get to know other pastors. Listen to their insights. What is the spiritual condition of other churches? How is the spiritual unity

among pastors? What issues do they feel hinder the work of the Kingdom in their area? Find your teammates, ask for their blessing as you join God's team in your area and pray with them!

As you get to know the area, prayerfully make a list of two main dynamics:

First, list the _spiritual strongholds_ (such as hopelessness, fear, poverty, self-righteousness, pleasure seeking, tradition, addiction, etc.) that identify the problems you must address to meet the needs of the people. A spiritual stronghold is an ingrained attitude of hopelessness based on a lie from Satan that keeps people bound in sin and separated from God.

Second, list the _redemptive gifts_ God wants to bless the area with...His possibilities! Ask the Lord to show you assets you can leverage for redemptive purposes. What ministries can you develop to meet people's needs and break strongholds? A redemptive gift is a supernatural release of power from God that brings His redemption to people, liberating those held captive by strongholds.

For example, if one of the strongholds in an area is addiction and hopelessness, some of the redemptive gifts the Lord might want to release to set captives free could include a grace-giving accepting community, deliverance, prayer, etc. Ministries that could be developed with those insights could include spiritually based 12 Step Groups, accountability relationships, prayer ministries and more.

The key principle here is: we develop our strategies and ministries based on what we discover in our mission field!

Check the "S*o*I*L" (Sphere of Influence Leaders)

Statistics are helpful and spiritual survey work is vital, but when we listen to real people, our ministry becomes uniquely personal. Get to know the _people_ of the community. Prayerfully walk among the people of your mission field, asking God to show you their needs through His eyes. Talk with the people of your mission field, humbly seeking friendships as one who wants to learn. As you do, the Lord will do amazing things! Listening enables us to discern where the Lord is already at work. Troy Evans, pastor of The Edge Church in Grand Rapids, Michigan, encourages us to "learn from indigenous wisdom."

Key missional questions we might ask as we study our mission field include:

- What needs does Jesus want us to meet to bring more people to know Him?
- What assets and relationships could the Lord use redemptively?
- Who knows what we need to know?
- What's not being done in our area that we could do?
- Who are the "persons of peace"?
- What could be our Kingdom niche and unique contribution to His work in this area?

As we listen, two kinds of people will be especially helpful: "Persons of Peace" (P*o*P) and Sphere of Influence Leaders (S*o*I*L). A person of peace is someone who has influence in the area whether they have a title or not. They can open doors to large networks of relationships, influence and opportunities to serve. A biblical example of a person of peace is Lydia in Acts 16:11-16. Finding persons of peace is essential!

There are other key leaders you'll want to listen to. Develop a list of the different kinds of sphere of influence leaders—in your mission field. Here are some examples of the different types of "S*o*I*L" in your area. You can add more to the list.

1. *Education*—school leaders
2. *Law Enforcement*—police chief, sheriff, etc.
3. *Government*—mayor, city/county officials, city planners, etc.
4. *Spiritual leaders*—pastors and other ministry leaders...our Kingdom teammates
5. *Business leaders*—Chamber of Commerce, Rotary, etc.
6. *Social service agencies*
7. *Media*—publishers, radio/TV, etc.
8. *Subcultures*—leaders in niche groups like partiers, bikers, ethnic groups, etc.
9. *Realtors and builders*
10. *"Community organizations"*— groups of people who meet because of a common interest such as Chamber of Commerce, Rotary, support groups, hobbies or other special interests
11. *Sports and recreation organizations*

12. The *"Bishop"*—the most influential spiritual leader of the area to learn from. Ask for their blessing
13. *"Divine appointments"*—watch for the people God sends to you
14. "Niche" groups who may be unique to your area

What are the names of the leaders represented by these spheres of influence? As you find out the name of each sphere of influence leader, pray for them! Pray for the Lord to help you find receptive "soil!"

Call the leaders on your list. Tell them that you and your church want to become a better servant to your community and you are interested in learning from them. Ask them if you could have about a half hour of their time. Often these kinds of leaders are pleasantly surprised when they meet church leaders who want to listen before they speak. Remember, be gracious and be brief. If they appear interested and want to give you more time, take advantage of their generosity and learn much.

Here's a sample survey you can use with these sphere of influence leaders.

1. How would you describe this area to a new person just moving in? What are our greatest strengths?
2. From your position as a leader of influence in this area, what do you see to be our biggest needs?
3. What are some ways a church that wants to be a servant to our area could partner with groups like yours to help others?
4. What advice would you give me as a spiritual leader in our community?
5. Who else would you recommend that I talk to that could help me learn more?
6. How can I pray for you or your family? How can we serve you?
7. Thank you for your time! May we keep you updated on our progress?

After you've done your "Check the S*O*I*L" interviews, bring your team together and pray about what you've learned. Glean the key issues from those conversations as indicators of how the Lord is leading you to engage your community redemptively.

COACH YOURSELF FORWARD

1. What did you learn from the demographic statistics about your mission field? Draw a "map" of your mission field capturing the main boundaries and key insights from those statistics.

2. As you look at the "spiritual map" of your area, what are the spiritual dynamics you need to address in prayer? How will you keep your intercessors informed and active?

3. What are the strongholds/needs of your mission field? What are some ways you can address them?

4. What are the redemptive gifts/ministry opportunities you are discovering? What are some ways you can activate them?

5. Draw a picture that describes the heart profile of the needs, values and dreams of the people of your mission field.

6. In light of what you have discovered and discerned, what types of ministries might you develop?

7. What kinds of teams will you need for those ministries?

FURTHER RESOURCES

Percept Ministries www.perceptgroup.com

EASI   www.easidemographics.com

Breaking the Missional Code, Ed Stetzer. B&H Academic, 2006.

Appendix C
"Statistical Insights"
"Spiritual Dynamics"
"Check the S*o*I*L"

Appendix D
"Spy Teams"

"Shaping"
Your Church for Missional Engagement

"Wow…we didn't know how much we didn't know…and we needed to know!" exclaimed Tom as he and Bill met at their next coaching visit.

"I can't wait to hear what our team's been learning and process those discoveries with you," said Bill. "Before we focus on our mission field here, I'm curious what you've been hearing from your ministry buddies. You told me that you have been sharing what we've been doing with them. How have they been adapting these principles and practices in their ministry settings?"

Tom leaned forward, smiling, "They've been really excited. You know how diverse their ministry environments are. Yet, it doesn't seem to matter whether they are urban, suburban, rural, small church, large church, new church or different country. They all tell me that because this isn't a one-size-fits-all program, they are developing and personalizing a game plan for their unique mission field." Tom grinned, "I've also been telling them the "Listen, Care, Celebrate…GROW" coaching path you've used with me. They've started using it with their leaders. We're starting to coach each other. It's fun! Coaching isn't as easy as you make it look, though. I need to learn more about how to coach."

"You're making good progress in your coaching skills. I'm glad your buddies are finding what we're doing is helpful for what they are doing," said Bill. "Thanks for the update. So what would you like to focus on today?"

"Well, like I said, we didn't know how much we needed to know until we decided to become students of our mission field," replied Tom. "There's so much we learned! There are so many needs! I want to discern what the Lord wants us to do with what we've learned. What needs are we supposed to address? What ministries should we develop? What does Jesus want us to do?"

"Great questions. Could I add another that might help us with our goal for today?" At Tom's affirmative nod, he continued, "What needs are you and your church best suited to meet?"

Tom sat thoughtfully. "That's a great question. I'm not sure. What's the best way to figure that out?"

"The Holy Spirit is very wise in the way He leads," said Bill. "We'll have to discern what needs He wants us to focus on in the community. At the same time, the ministry He wants us to do outside the church will also fit who He's brought together *inside* our church body. So...let's see how He's shaped our church to meet the needs of our mission field. My friend and fellow missionary Paul Ford likes to say, 'Let's see who God has brought to see what God intends.'"

"So...it will be a blend of what we've learned about our mission field and what we learn about ourselves," Tom said.

"Right. Let's get the picture of the needs that consistently rose to the surface in our study. That helps us sense what needs the Lord is telling us to address. We can't minister to all the needs out there, but there are some that the Lord wants us to meet that fit who we are."

Tom pulled out a paper and spread it out so they could both see it. "Here's the synthesis of what we've learned. The S*o*I*L interviews were especially helpful." He pointed to a short list on the page, "These needs are the ones that we heard consistently. We've been praying especially about them."

"Great work," commented Bill. He pulled out a fresh piece of paper. "Let's see how those needs fit who we are as a church." He wrote "Mission Field Needs" on one side of the page and "Our Ministry Strengths" on the other side, forming two columns. "Let's write the needs the Lord is highlighting for us and then see how He might use our gifts and skills to meet them."

"We've done some study of spiritual gifts in our church," commented Tom, "But I'm afraid to say we looked at gifts more from the perspective of ministry in the Body than from engaging our mission field."

"Knowing how the power of God works in and through us is vital," said Bill. "Our ministry profile helps shape our ministries. We bear fruit best when we fit and flourish in ministry." Bill smiled at Tom, "Where do you best fit and flourish?"

"Fit and flourish...what do you mean by that?" asked Tom.

"Well, there are different ways to say it," said Bill. "Some call it their 'sweet spot.' Another way to describe it is identifying when you most often experience God's power, joy and fruit in your life. Another way is to say it's your ministry fit. Where you fit and flourish is a blend of a number of factors."

"I understand. What would those factors be?" asked Tom.

Bill's eyes twinkled and he smiled, "What factors do you think are important?"

Tom grinned. "Ok, Coach. Let's coach ourselves and see what we can come up with."

Together Bill and Tom compiled a list of ways Tom could describe and clarify his sweet spot. It included "natural wiring" (personality and leadership style), supernatural empowerment (spiritual gifts), competencies (talents and learned skills), life experiences, successes and ministry burdens/passions. They reviewed again Tom's interests and hobbies that could be leveraged more redemptively.

Tom's face showed his excitement. "This is great! I wish someone would have helped me understand where I fit and flourish earlier. It would have made a big difference in how I used my time and energy."

Tom paused for a moment. "I love this list, but how can I learn about these areas? Is there some kind of test I'm supposed to take?"

"Great question," responded Bill. "The way I like to think about 'fit and flourish' is that it's not a test you take that you can pass or fail, but a process of discernment that affirms how the Lord made and shaped you. We use some ministry profile tools as the base for our discerning process."

"I like the process you describe," Tom said. "There have been too many times in my life where I felt like I was asked to do something just because a job needed to be done without any real concern for whether I actually was suited to do it well. I was just an available warm body. Come to think of it, I do that too often when I ask people in our church to serve. If they show any kind of willingness, I tend to plug them in whether they fit or not. The results of that approach for our people as individuals and teams have been," he said with a grimace, "less than effective."

Bill nodded. "That's common in many organizations, including churches and mission agencies. But it doesn't need to be that way. Our most precious resource is the people God trusts us with. He wants us to steward our lives well so we can fit and flourish and make our best contribution for eternity. For spiritual leaders like us, it's our privilege and responsibility to help others fit and flourish, too."

Tom was thoughtful for a moment. "So...let's talk about the profiles, especially personality and spiritual gifts. First, I have a concern and then a question."

"Ok, what's your concern?" asked Bill.

"Well, sometimes I didn't have a positive experience in the past taking some kind of profile. I felt like I was taking a test and my score put me in a box or pigeon-holed me. I almost wondered if some of the information could be used against me. There's more to me than a score on a piece of paper!"

Bill nodded. "I certainly understand that concern. I have felt that way at times, too. That's why a good profile is only part of the overall fit and flourish process. May I share some thoughts about what our process is not and what it is supposed to be?"

Tom nodded with interest. "Sure."

Bill pulled out a piece of paper and wrote in two columns:

The profile and process is NOT...	The profile and process IS...
1. A way to put you in a box or pigeon hole you	1. A process to help you see and steward who you are
2. An excuse for unhealthy or sinful behavior	2. A way to help you express needs in a healthy way
3. A test you pass or fail	3. Designed to stimulate conversation and discovery
4. The last word on your identity	4. Dependent on the Spirit's guidance and grace—His purifying and maturing work
5. Only about you	5. About you, your team and Kingdom ministry

Tom studied the two columns for a moment. "I'm much more comfortable with that approach. Now onto my question... what kind of profile do you recommend?"

Bill smiled. "I have one that I like best. Over the years, I've become a student of these kinds of profiles. From my perspective, there's one that is by far the most comprehensive and helpful. It actually helps you see both natural personality and spiritual gifts. It's called the Grip-Birkman."

"Grip-Birkman...hmmm, quite a name. Tell me about it."

Bill smiled again. "The Grip-Birkman actually blends two distinct profiles into one overall process. The Birkman Method is one of the premier personality or behavioral profiles available. It's been done by over four million people around the world. It gives you the best in-depth look at our personality or what I call our natural wiring. The 'Grip' is short for 'Your Leadership Grip,' a spiritual gifts inventory developed by Paul Ford. It helps you get the best overall look or fresh 'grip' on your spiritual gifts or the supernatural side of things."

"Sounds interesting," replied Tom. "What makes them so good?"

"Let's start with the Birkman profile," Bill said. "This assessment focuses on your natural interests and personality, showing the way you act relationally with others. It is more in-depth overall than any other profile yet can be accessed in different smaller segments. For example one segment called the Life Style Grid helps me identify four key issues: my underlying motivation—what interests and nourishes me, my usual or effective style, my underlying needs—the support or environment I need to be effective, and my stress response when those needs are not met. The two underlying areas—motivation and needs—are so important because others can't see them. The Birkman gives us language to share them in healthy, gracious ways so we can work with others more effectively. It also goes deeper and wider than any other tool of its kind, which is really is helpful in digging deeper to understand your behaviors."

"Wow...those kinds of insights would make a huge difference in how I would work with others," Tom said.

"It has for me," replied Bill. "And that's just one segment of the overall profile!"

"What about the spiritual gifts profile you mentioned?" asked Tom.

"It's called 'Your Leadership Grip,'" said Bill. "It takes you farther in understanding your spiritual gifts than any other profile. It shows how you are powerful in the Spirit beyond your natural personality."

"How so?" asked Tom

Your Leadership Grip Triangle

Your Spiritual Gifts

Equipping or
Supporting Gifts...
or a Combination?

Do you lead most effectively
"Upfront" or "Alongside"...
or both?

Your Team Styles
(How your gifts function
in a team setting)

Body Building Roles
(How God uses your gifts to
fulfill His redemptive mission)

Bill drew a triangle on a piece of paper. "Your Leadership Grip helps you look at your spiritual gifts—the power of God above and beyond your personality—from three different angles. We look at your gift triangle from these perspectives. Each angle gives you a different 'handle' or 'grip' on how your gifts actually function. First, you look at your gift mix and identify if your gifts are more equipping—God's power shows through your words— or supporting—God's power shows up through your actions as you serve.

"Second, you look at your Team Styles—how your gifts function in a team. We see if God's power is more evident when you are up in front of people or alongside people...or both. Third, you look at what we call your Body Building Roles—how God stewards your gifts to accomplish His Great Commission redemptive purposes. We look at where you are strong and also who you need, making sure to have both an 'I' and a 'We' view of our gifts. When you put together both the natural and the supernatural, you have a great way to see how God has designed you to live out His calling in your life...to fit and flourish."

Tom's eyes were bright with interest. "Why hasn't anyone shared something like this with me before? Could you help me walk through the Grip-Birkman profile?"

Bill nodded in return. "I'd be glad to. It's a key part of the overall fit and flourish process. If you like it, you might want me to take some of your leaders through the process, too."

Two weeks later, Tom and Bill met again.

"Ok, I've received my Grip-Birkman results and have read

through my profile. Wow! There's a lot here. How do I make the most of all this good information?" Tom asked.

Bill smiled. "Welcome to another use for coaching. You can use basic coaching skills to come alongside and empower anyone, anywhere, anytime about anything. When you are coaching someone around the results of a tool or other kind of special process, we call it specialization coaching. We're going to use our basic coaching skills to unpack the specific information of your Grip-Birkman profile."

"So...are we limited to the numbers of my profile results, or can interact with them more as we coach?" Tom asked. "How do you coach someone when they have specific scores on a profile like this?"

Bill nodded in approval. "Good question. We've developed a simple way to go beyond the numbers to get a better picture of your reality. It's a coaching process I call 'Four Passes of Sober Estimation' based on Romans 12:3."

Tom's eyes showed interest. "Tell me more."

Bill's eyes twinkled in return. "Romans 12 is a tremendous ministry passage. Verses one and two tell us that in view of God's mercy, the most reasonable thing we can do is give our lives completely to Him. As we do, He transforms us by renewing our minds. Verse three says to make a sober estimation or honest evaluation of who we are. From there the passage beautifully gives guidance about using our gifts and stewarding our relationships. That's why just getting the number score on a profile of some kind is only a part of our honest evaluation of who we are. The four passes help us get a fuller picture."

Tom leaned forward. "What are the four passes? How do they fit into our coaching process?" He pushed his notepad across the table to Bill. "Write them down for me, coach...if you please."

"Glad to," said Bill as he began to write.

Four Passes of Sober Estimation
1. Review the results
2. Reflect on your experiences
3. Received feedback
4. Revelation of the Spirit

"Whenever you coach someone through a profile like this, their score is the starting point of getting to the best picture of reality. Both the Birkman and Your Leadership Grip profiles are very good...they paint in most of the picture."

Tom nodded. "I felt like they were both pretty much on target. So did my wife. She told me that she'd been telling me these things for years!"

Bill laughed and nodded. "My wife did, too! We both ought to listen to them better...but don't tell her I admitted that!"

Tom chuckled. "I won't if you won't."

Bill pointed back to the notepad. "Ok, back to business. Our first pass is to review what the profile results tell us. As I said, they are very helpful. Make sure you understand what their definitions are.

"Our second pass is to reflect on your experiences. Take the score off the paper and make it personal. What does this look like in your life? How often does it happen? What stories could you share that would be an example?"

Tom nodded thoughtfully. "I like that principle...take the score off the paper and make it personal. Now I see where this is leading What about the other two passes?"

Bill continued, "Our third pass is what I call 'received feedback.' What have others said *to* you or *about* you that give us further insight? The confirmation and affirmation of others is very helpful.

"Our fourth pass is what I call 'revelation of the Spirit.' Sometimes our scores just don't seem to fit us. Then we lay things before the Lord and ask for His wisdom. Revelation from Him gives us insights we can't get anywhere else."

Tom tapped the words on the notepad. "Now *this* really makes sense to me. Using these four passes will give us the fullest picture of who we are. Great stuff!"

"Thank you," Bill responded humbly.

"How do the four passes blend in with the coaching process?" Tom asked.

"The four passes all fit into our 'R' in the GROW," said Bill. As we get blend the content of a profile into the context of our life, we get clarity—insights and discovery. From there we can coach people to discover their options and develop action steps."

"How would that work with my Grip-Birkman profile?" Tom asked.

"Let's coach ourselves around something in your profile," Bill replied. "For example, I love to start coaching people through their Grip-Birkman profiles starting with what I call the 'Natural Me' reports—Birkman Areas of Interest and the Birkman Lifestyle Grid. Let's look at your Areas of Interest. Birkman helps you identify activities that either energize or drain you. ' They measure ten areas on a scale from 1 to 99. The higher the score, the more you gain energy from those areas. They fill your tank, nourish you and are good for you. Anything above 90 is more than just an interest...it's a genuine need. Conversely, the lower scores represent areas that may drain you. Anything below 10 is an area to avoid. Good stewardship would lead you to be intentional about doing things that energize you and delegate areas that drain you...especially to people who would be nourished by them. What do you notice about your scores?"

Tom looked over his Areas of Interest and read not only the scores but the definitions about them. "Hmmm," he mused. "I have a 97 on Literary, which makes a lot of sense. I love to read, and the power of using the right words to communicate is important to me. On the lower scores I notice that I have a nine on Clerical...that is so true! Details and data management drain me."

Bill nodded. "So...what do those two areas look like for you? How much time do you spend doing them?"

Tom pondered for a moment, growing realization showing on his face. "I don't spend enough time on the Literary. I feel like I'm missing something when I don't have time to read. And...I'm spending too much time doing Clerical things. That stuff really drains me!"

"Good insights...you've taken the Birkman content and personalized it. You've received insight and clarity about that information. Now...what options and action steps would you like to develop to address those discoveries?"

"I know what comes next!" Tom grinned. "Let's coach to some action steps."

They did.

"So, that's a taste of coaching the Birkman," Tom said. "Could we taste something from the Leadership Grip?"

"Sure!" Bill turned to the "Your Leadership Grip" summary page. "I've already described the three angles of our gifts triangle. We're asking three main questions as we interact with your results—'Where is God powerful through me? How I am I weak? Who do I need?' When we look at your Team Styles, for example, we want to identify the two team styles where you are strong because of your gifts and who you need on a team with you. What do you see on your profile?"

Tom looked intently at his profile for a moment. "It says that my two strongest scores are 'Let's Go' and 'Let Me Help You' and the style I need most is 'Let's Be Careful.' So, if we use our Four Passes of Sober Estimation, we should get insights that we could use to coach me to some action steps, right?"

"Right," replied Bill. "Let's do that. One more thing you can do...you can blend how you describe your team styles. In your case, you might say your best team style is 'Let Me Help You Go.' God's gifts are His power...not a list of separate gifts, but a mix of gifts that complement and cooperate with each other to make the Spirit's power so amazing. Think about that as we coach through your team styles."

As they did, Tom was affirmed by how God used His gifts when he worked with others. He also realized how much he needed a particular "Let's Be Careful" person who had been irritating him because their approach to things was quite different than his.

"Whew!" Tom exhaled. "The person I need most is that one I had been struggling with! I'm going to let them know how much I need them and appreciate them on our team."

"Irritate or appreciate...the choice is yours," Bill returned with a smile. "That principle has made a huge difference for me. It's also helped me understand how healthy teams form. At first we may say, 'I *have* to be on a team with you. Then we may acknowledge, 'I *need* you on my team. However, our goal for healthy missional teams can be when people say to each other, 'I *want* to be on a team with you."

Tom nodded somberly. I can see how the results of a great profile tool like the Grip-Birkman can make a huge difference in how we develop ministry teams, how we live life in biblical community, and how we work together most effectively to fulfill the Great Commandment. Now I can see why 'fit and flourish' leadership development is so crucial."

Bill nodded in agreement, "Paul Ford says that we should give at least two-thirds of our time in ministry where we fit and flourish. If we don't, it will drain us and we'll burn out quickly. We won't be as fruitful, and we may hinder someone else from serving where they are most effective."

A look of realization came across Tom's face. "I'm spending too much time where I'm not effective. I need to adjust my ministry so I can give the majority of my energy to my strengths. Beyond that, I need to help others do that too. Imagine how powerful our church would be if our people were all equipped and released in ministries where they fit and flourished!"

"Now you've got it. How could you do that?"

Tom grinned knowingly. "Let's coach ourselves to a game plan for that."

They did.

"Way to go!" Bill said as they reviewed Tom's action steps. "May I add one more dimension to what we just did?" At Tom's nod, Bill said, "We've just helped you and your people know how to discover where they fit and flourish. How can we do the same thing for the church corporately so that we match our strengths with our mission field's needs?"

"Good thought," said Tom. "We've covered a lot of ground today. Do you mind taking some more time? I'd like to bring all these things together so I can take them back to our leadership team at church and work this through with them."

"Let's go for it," agreed Bill. By the time they'd finished, Tom had a game plan that addressed several vital areas:

1. Tom would adjust his schedule so he could invest more time where he fit and flourished, paying even more attention to leveraging his life redemptively.
2. Tom would work with his leaders to help them discover where they would best fit and flourish.
3. Their church would do a ministry profile to help leverage its strengths and address some areas of concern.
4. They would discern how to match the needs of their mission field with their strengths as a church, staying sensitive to the leading of the Spirit as they developed teams.
5. Tom would share his notes with his ministry friends so they could adapt them for their use.

"Whew...we made great progress, but there's a lot of work ahead. I feel like the pieces are coming together though. It makes me even more dependent on the Lord than ever!" exclaimed Tom.

Bill nodded. "That's a wonderful place to live...desperately dependent on Jesus! It reminds me of a verse that has encouraged me many times from Philippians 2:13, 'For it is God who works in you both to will and to act in order to fulfill His good purpose.'"

"Let's claim that as we pray," said Tom. They did.

Let Your Mission Field and Your Ministry Teams Shape Your Strategy

We've been learning that a church's vision often starts in the hearts of its leaders but is shaped by its mission field as well. As the gifts and skills of your team or ministry help define how you impact others powerfully, you can let you mission field shape the vision and ministry strategies of your church. Here are some key ideas to make this happen:

First, if the number of people in your mission field who are unchurched is about 80 percent (based on research by David Olson in *The American Church in Crisis*), how many people does that represent in the geographic area the Lord has made you responsible for? Learn the percentage of people who don't know Jesus in your area. By faith, what percent of those people will you claim for Christ? For example, if there are 10,000 people in your mission field, about 8,000 of them are currently unchurched. If you claimed one percent of them for Christ, your goal would be to see 80 people become disciples of Jesus. If you become a five percent church, you'd be claiming 400 people to come to Christ. What is the Lord calling you to claim?

Second, estimate how many people your church has the potential to touch tangibly with the love of Jesus. Consider both the ministries of your church and the influence of your people where they live and work. How many people is the Lord inviting you to touch with His love?

Third, when you blend the redemptive opportunities of your mission field with your church's sweet spots and strengths, how does that further shape your vision?

1. How many people in your mission field are unchurched? (Hint: the national average in the United States is about 80 percent of the population in your area, but you should be able to be more specific based on your own local research.)

2. How many of that number is the Lord inviting you to claim? How many will become new disciples of Jesus because of your ministry? One percent? Five percent? Ten percent?

3. How many people are within the "sphere of influence" of the people of your church? How many people could your church touch at least once a year with the love of Jesus in some practical way?

4. How can you incorporate these ministry goals into your intercession strategy?

Learn How You Fit and Flourish—Both I/Me and We!

It is wonderful when we lead people to discovery and clarity about how they best fit and flourish! We have already begin to think about the natural and supernatural ways that God has designed you. These are central elements to your Game Plan that reveal their sweet spot or ministry profile. Key elements so far are that are revealed in the Grip-Birkman discovery reports:

1. *Natural wiring*—your personality—what energizes you, drains you, how you process information and relate to people, the environment and support you need to be effective.
2. *Personal skills and hobbies*—what you're good at and what's good for you.
3. *Supernatural empowerment*—spiritual gifts: God's power above and beyond your personality.

Let's add three other parts of who you are that may reveal even more depth of how God has prepared you to impact others:

4. *Fruit*—effectiveness, past successes and fruitfulness
5. *Passion*—ministry burden or vision
6. *History*—life experiences the Lord can use for redemptive purposes

Not only is it important to help each person develop their ministry profile, it's important to see how our individual sweet spots come together to form God's team. Veteran missionary Dr. Paul Ford of CRM reminds us that we must pay attention to both "me" and "we" in understanding how the body of Christ can be healthy and effective in missional ministry.

Your Leadership Grip and *Discovering Your Ministry Identity* by Paul Ford help people see their spiritual gifts from three angles—their gift mix, how their gifts function in a team setting and how their gifts function in the Body of Christ for redemptive purposes. *Discovering Your Ministry Identity* is often called "the poor man's Birkman" because of its affordability. Learn more at www.gripbirkman.com

Assess Your Team Collectively

The Grip-Birkman discovery reports also work very well as a framework for discerning how God has prepared your team or your ministry. It is equally important to evaluate your leadership team and your church or ministry to know where you are healthy and where you need to address some concerns. The Grip-Birkman **Team Builders Toolkit**, available at www.churchsmart.com, gives a simple way to move from I to WE in the process of creating a more intentional body life ministry among your people. There are many congregational health tools that are helpful such as the Natural Church Development (NCD) process. Learn more about NCD at that same www.churchsmart.com.

Profile Your Ministry Missionally

However, beyond the tools to be used to do profiles of your ministry team(s) or your whole church or ministry, some essential elements have to be in place for a missional church health process to be effective.

First, be clear about the purpose for the process. There has to be clarity about our mission that produces passion and urgency. *Our primary purpose is to "follow the Great Commandment and fulfill the Great Commission."* Our singular aspiration is summed up in the words of Jesus: "The Son of Man has come to seek and save the lost...and give them life to the fullest" (Luke 19:10; John 10:10). *Our focus must be on making disciples who make disciples.* A missional health process requires wise, courageous leadership!

The leaders of the church must commit to a process that will take place over a period of months, not just getting the scores of a profile or doing an event. Willingness to be accountable through the process from the very beginning is essential.

Second, do a comprehensive profile of your church. The goal is to get a clear picture of the church that includes input from external and objective sources as well as the personal insights of the church people. Do an *objective evaluation* with a tool such as NCD. Get *onsite input* from leaders and people of the church to help "paint the picture."

If you choose to do an onsite evaluation led by an outside specialist or team, look at issues such as your ministry's history, facilities, attendance and financial statistics, the church's mission field, policies and insights from church members. Share the *written profile* results with pastor, leaders and people. The results should be a *clear picture of reality* with strengths to celebrate and issues to address; recommendations with *clear outcomes that will translate into goals*; and responses and *commitments by the pastor, leaders and people to see the process through to completion*. Paul Borden has written several books that speak to these kinds of issues as well.

Third, develop practical steps for implementation. As you process the information,

- *Further personalize the recommendations by developing clear outcomes and goals all tied to your mission and mission field*. Your game plan should celebrate and leverage strengths and also address key areas of concern or "minimum factors."

- *Develop both a Church Health Plan and a Missional Game Plan* to engage your mission field. "Health" and "harvest" go together!

- *Empower Prayer and Health Teams*. Keep your intercessors informed and active!

- Empower your missional health team to work with your leadership team. Clearly communicate who has the ability to make recommendations and decisions.

- *The process needs to be pastor-led and supported and protected by district or judicatory leaders.*

- *Coaching is essential. Incorporate training throughout the process* to equip leaders to reach missional goals.

- Determine to go through this kind of missional health process every year or two as part of the regular rhythm of life as a church or ministry.

Assessing leaders and churches so they know where they best fit and flourish is a vital part of developing a missional game plan!

COACH YOURSELF FORWARD

1. The ministry of assessment is a key part of our Game Plan. How will you develop ways to help individuals in your church know how they can best fit and flourish?

2. How will you develop a plan to assess your church's collective health? How will you make sure it is integrated into a missional game plan?

3. How will you integrate coaching into your assessing and equipping process?

Link Community Needs with Your Church's Gifts and Strengths

Connecting the gifts and skills the Lord has given your team with the needs of your mission field takes a blend of both spiritual and strategic wisdom. Prayerfully list the needs and opportunities of your mission field alongside the strengths and sweet spots of your church. Keeping in mind the gifts of key individuals that are active in ministry will enable you to get very specific. But don't limit yourself to a few; think of the strengths of the rest of the Body as well—if there is a way to do that. Remember Paul Ford says, *"Let's see who God has brought to us to see what God intends to do through us."* Here are some questions to help you process these issues.

- What have we learned from checking the S*o*I*L?
- What needs does Jesus want us to meet?
- What assets and opportunities are in the community that we could leverage for redemptive purposes?
- What ministry teams do we have in our church that could address those needs?

- What mission teams could we develop to bring Good News to our community?
- What kinds of leaders will we need for these teams?

Develop a side-by-side list of the "Needs and Opportunities of Our Mission Field" with the "Strengths and Sweet Spots of Our Church."

There are many things your church *could* do...ask the Lord what *He* wants you to do! Veteran coach and missionary Steve Ogne offers three good questions for discerning what missional activities to invest in:

1. How well does this activity make a difference by meeting real needs?
2. How well does this activity help us build relationships?
3. How well does this activity help us make disciples?

Empower Ministry and Mission Teams

Remember, our first goal is to equip every disciple in our fellowship to live as a missionary in their world. Individuals building redemptive bridges in their spheres of influence set the stage for the Body of Christ to ministry corporately through teams.

Now consider the teams needed for the ministries your church will develop. There are two kinds of teams to consider: current *ministry teams* already in your church that could become more missional and *mission teams* that will allow even more people to get involved in ministry outside your church.

When it comes to your church's current ministry, look at them from three key perspectives:

1. Which ministries help your people go deep with God?
2. Which help your people go deep with others?
3. Which ministries help your people go deep into the Harvest...how many are missional?

Veteran ministry leaders Steve Ogne and Chip Arn both estimate that the average church has 10-15 teams that do ministry in the church for every one team that does ministry outside the church. How can you become more balanced?

Think about how to make your existing ministries more intentionally missional. For example, the worship team could begin doing music sets at a local coffee place. Your hospitality team could serve lunch to area business leaders or teachers at a local school. Your nursery and children's ministry teams could do a "Parent's Night Out" that allows moms and dads some time for a date or shopping while the church ministers to their kids. There are many creative ways that ministry teams can become more effective relational bridges to your community while building up those already in the Body of Christ.

External Mission Teams focus on serving the needs and opportunities of our mission field. As they do, they provide new possibilities for people to get involved. There are untapped and underutilized people resources in your church and community! Prayerfully develop a list of new teams you can deploy in your missional game plan.

For a worksheet to develop your ministry and mission teams, see Appendix C.

Look for Team Leaders

There is a lot of good information available today about leadership and teams. Raising up and equipping leaders for your ministry and mission teams an essential part of multiplying your ministry effectiveness. Who you choose to invest your time in is a crucial issue. Here's a simple way to categorize different kinds of people in your church:

"Moochers" drain time and energy. They often have special needs that require healing before they can contribute to the mission. Develop ministries for them where they can learn to help each other, such as support groups. As they heal, they will contribute instead of drain.

"Members" are nice people who attend and often appreciate what you do, but don't contribute much to the mission. They may be waiting to be invited to find how they can fit and flourish and contribute to the mission. Don't assume they are not interested in ministry. Find the key to their heart and open the door for them to get involved in a way that they are passionate about .

"Ministers" are willing to serve and have abilities in particular areas. They make great members of a team or can do a specific ministry well.

"Multipliers" have the capacity to recruit others to a vision, equip them, build teams and multiply themselves. They are rare and an essential resource to expand God's work!

"Missionaries" can contribute for a short season in specific ways. They may come to your church to help, but not feel led to stay long

term. These leaders are especially important in starting new churches. Your church may also send out missionaries to help ministries outside your church locally or even globally!

As you consider the human resources in your church and the teams you need, look especially for multipliers! These people are like diamonds...fairly rare and very valuable. Learn to look for potential multipliers... sometimes there are diamonds in the rough just waiting to be encouraged and equipped among the people of your church (young and old). Ask the Lord to help you see them!

COACH YOURSELF FORWARD

1. List the ministries of your church according to the three areas we identified:
   a. Ministries that help your people go deep with God.
   b. Ministries that help your people go deep with each other.
   c. Ministries that help your people go deep into the harvest.

   As you reviewed your ministries from these perspectives, what do you notice? How balanced are your ministries? What might you need to adjust? How can you view all your ministries through a missional lens in order to align them with God's missional purposes?

2. Comparing the needs of your mission field with the strengths of your church, what connections and possibilities did you see? What is the Holy Spirit prioritizing for you?

3. As we look at your existing ministry teams and potential mission teams, how can they be better aligned with your missional game plan? How could these teams partner with existing groups or organizations outside your church?

4. In what ways can your current ministry teams become more missional? What might you need to stop doing so you can start doing ministry according to the Holy Spirit's priorities?

5. How will you bring together the new teams you need for missional ministries? Who are your ministers and multipliers? How will you equip and release them?

6. As you look at the people of your church, who does the Holy Spirit want you to invest in? Who is outside your

church that could be invited to be part of one of your teams?

7. Who are the younger leaders God is raising up? How might you include them?

FURTHER RESOURCES

Doing Church as a Team by Wayne Corderio. Regal, 2009.
Knocking Over the Leadership Ladder by Paul Ford. ChurchSmart, 2006.
Moving from I to We: Recovering the Biblical Vision for Stewarding the Church by Dr. Paul R. Ford. ChurchSmart, 2013.
The Birkman Method: Your Personality at Work by Sharon Birkman Fink and Stephanie Capparell. Jossey-Bass, 2013.
Grip-Birkman Profile www.gripbirkman.com
Natural Church Development process www.churchsmart.com

Appendix C
"Ministry Focus Group" profile
"Ministry Audit"
"Mission and Ministry Teams"
"Discerning Your Ministry Passion"

"Serving"
That Meets Needs and Opens Doors

As he did with each coaching visit, Bill took time to listen, care and celebrate with Tom about what was going on in his life. He checked in with Tom about his walk with Jesus, how his family was doing, how things were going at church and progress made on his action steps from their last visit.

"I appreciate how you take time to see how I'm doing when we meet," Tom commented. "I know we are working on ministry issues, but I can tell that as my coach you care about me personally, not just about bottom line performance."

"Glad you noticed," said Bill. "Coaching is a holistic relationship that cares about the person, not just the projects they are working on. Remember, our goal as coaches is to come alongside leaders so they are transformed into the image of Jesus

Coaches pay attention to the leader's "4 C's":
Clarifying calling
Cultivating character
Creating community
Connecting to culture

and join Him on His redemptive mission. That brings the Great Commandment and the Great Commission together in all we do. When we get together, I'm paying attention to what I call the "Four C's": clarifying calling, cultivating character, creating community and connecting to culture."

"What we've been doing recently has sure made a big difference in clarifying my calling," replied Tom. "What a difference it makes, living out my call where I fit and flourish! I've been thrilled to see the response of our people as we help them discover where they best fit and flourish. As they realize how Jesus designed them to make a unique contribution to His kingdom purposes, the level of excitement and engagement in our church is increasing in wonderful ways."

"It all fits together, doesn't it?" said Bill. "As we see the mission field through the Father's eyes, we are connected to a great, compelling vision and mission. When we clarify our call so we understand that we all have a place on God's team, we appreciate each other more and create healthy community. When we join Jesus on His mission and see people's lives transformed, it fuels us and keeps us fresh. A church full of people that know who they are, why they're here and where they're going is contagious!"

"That's what we're finding out," returned Tom. "We hear more and more stories of how God is at work in neighborhoods, schools, workplaces, playgrounds...far beyond just inside our church building! There have been lots of bumps along the way, but knowing that Jesus is using us to change people's lives both now and forever makes it worth it. It also keeps us praying and dependent on Him!"

"We can't do anything without the purifying, maturing and empowering work of the Holy Spirit, that's for sure," Bill said. "What do you want to focus on today?"

"We've made great progress in understanding the needs of our mission field and the ways our church can develop ministries to meet those needs," said Tom. "We're getting clear about the *why* of our mission and the *who* and *what* of our mission field. Now we're trying to figure out the *how* and *when*. We want our people living missionally and making redemptive friendships, not just approaching people as a "project." We also want to be intentional about how we join Jesus on His mission corporately. We've had some people asking about how our current ministries fit into all this, especially our Sunday morning services. There's been some interesting conversation about how to connect ministry outside our church with what we are already doing inside. We are realizing that the bridges we are building have to create a flow of relationships in two ways—for us to go to our community and for them to come to us. We need to work on being more intentional about those bridges."

"You have been doing a good job of discerning what needs you are best suited to meet and who the Lord is sending you to serve," Bill commented. "How can you be more intentional about when you will serve and who you will serve with? Those issues involve designing a missional calendar and discerning who your missional partners might be. As you work on those issues, we'll discover more ways to develop the missional bridges you mentioned."

Tom nodded thoughtfully, "Connecting...living a missional lifestyle...Calendar, partners, bridges...those sound like key issues to focus on. Let's figure out a game plan to wisely meets needs and opens doors. Let's see how the Lord leads us today!"

Developing a Missional Lifestyle

Michael Frost, in his book *Exiles*, shares a simple but very effective approach to living a more intentional lifestyle or "missional rhythm," in his words, using the acronym "B*E*L*L*S." Here's an adaptation of his concept in order to *"live sent"*...

John 17:17-18
Jesus prayed, "Sanctify them by Your truth, Your word is truth. As You have sent Me into the world, I have sent them into the world."

Genesis 12:2,3
I will bless you...and you will be a blessing...and in you all the families of the earth will be blessed.

Romans 12:1-2 (The Message)
So here's what I want you to do, God helping you: Take your everyday, ordinary life—your sleeping, eating, going-to-work and walking-around life—and place it before God as an offering.

Bless at least 3 people each week
*This can be done many ways, but the key is to be intentional. "Blessing" could be an e-mail of affirmation or encouragement, mowing a neighbor's lawn or babysitting for a single mom. It could be a small gift, an act of service or acting as an agent of peace. Bless a person who is a believer. Bless a person who is not a professing Christian. As you've already been using the "B*L*E*S*S" strategy as you pray for people (see our section on intercession), you are now demonstrating God's love in practical ways intentionally.*

Eat with at least 3 other people each week
Eat with a person who is a believer. Eat with a person who is not a professing Christian. Leverage your meal times or coffee breaks for relational investment.

Listen to the promptings of God
Commit to specific times of solitude for active listening to God. Find the ways that you best connect to the Lord and hear His voice. Make it a part of your daily rhythm, especially in the "spaces" during your day. Give at least one hour each week for this activity.

Learn from the Gospels each week
Read the whole Bible...learn God's story! Have regular rhythm of

Bible study. However, take time to specifically read the Gospels in order to learn specifically from Jesus' ways and words.

Share Story

As we spend time with people, we will learn their stories. In their stories we will learn the keys to their hearts and discern how God is working in their lives. Wisely share your own story in ways that connect to their story. Weave in the Good News of God's Story as the Spirit leads. Learn a simple, clear way to present the Gospel so people can respond to the invitation of Jesus to follow Him.

At the end of your day, reflect these two questions...make them a matter of prayer...share them with your accountability partners: In what ways did I cooperate with Jesus today? In what ways did I resist Jesus today?

My friend Phil Newell has a similar approach using the acronym "L*O*V*E." His missional rhythm is:

> "Listen and Learn from God...so I can share with others.
>
> Offer a blessing...affirm others for who they are.
>
> Voice a prayer...link arms with others in their struggles and joys.
>
> Eat together...discover the sacredness of "breaking bread" with others."

Design a Missional Calendar

As leaders discern needs in their community, they must develop ways to demonstrate God's love by meeting those needs in practical, tangible ways in order to gain credibility for their message. Just like a missionary, we have to "earn the right to be heard" in the culture we live in! Rather than only trying to create events to invite people to attend (attractional), we find events and venues where people already are and find ways to serve there (missional). We must be intentional about bridging our service to more opportunities for ministry connections. A key principle is *"Where people congregate, we will operate."*

Watch for God's divine appointments and open doors. Ask how you can help and find ways to serve in your community. Then, go... love...serve! As you do, God will give you favor and relationships with people. Listen to their story. Learn more about those needs.

Keep serving them in love and you'll find spiritual conversations happening naturally...and supernaturally!

But What About Sunday?

Most pastors, especially those who lead smaller churches, live with the reality of their regular pastoral and administrative duties. Keeping missional priorities and activities are essential...it's too easy to experience what some call "mission drift." That's what makes ongoing coaching so important.

It's common for church planters and pastors to ask about how regular church activities, especially Sunday services, fit into a missional game plan. In reality, churches spend most of their energy on their Sunday experience...Sunday School classes, children's church and especially on a worship service. What we do on Sunday is necessary, but not sufficient for a missional game plan. We often put almost all our disciple-making eggs into one Sunday basket! We have to expand the ways we are building redemptive bridges so we can make disciples who make disciples.

A word picture borrowed from Steve Ogne and Dave DeVries illustrates this point well. In the game of chess, the most powerful piece on the board is the queen. Many inexperienced players rely heavily on the queen, using it as the primary piece to win the game. However, there are many other pieces on the board that are also important. A good chess player learns to use all the pieces as part of a winning game plan. Sometimes novice chess players are encouraged to learn to play without the queen. When they learn to use the other pieces well, it makes the queen even more powerful as part of a comprehensive game plan. In essence, in order to really play chess well, you first have to learn to play without the queen.

From a church ministry perspective, the "queen" is our Sunday morning worship service. We tend to overuse the queen! When we try to make our Sunday morning worship services accomplish everything--evangelism, worship, discipleship, teaching and fellowship--we are not using the other pieces on our board. It's important to have a great Sunday experience that translates the Good News for new people (more about that later), but it's even more important to build bridges out into the community that make it easier for people to come into church. Remember, an effective game plan is both missional and attractional, but makes being missional the priority.

If you are a planting a church, there will be a lot of pressure to "start having church," which means "start having Sunday morning services." Focusing too much on Sunday can hinder you from equipping your people to be out in the community making disciples through missional lifestyles and ministries. Learn to play without the queen—don't start Sunday services too soon. Utilize the other pieces on your board—making disciples through strategic prayer, incarnating the Gospel through service, relationship building, creating small groups or missional communities, checking the "S*o*I*L" and living a missional lifestyle. Then, when you add the "queen"—your Sunday morning ministries, you'll do it as part of a comprehensive missional game plan.

If you are pastoring an existing church, help people see that a missional game plan will add to your effectiveness, not take away from what you are already doing. Your goal will be to make sure that what you do on Sunday is integrated into what you are doing the rest of the week out in your community. If you do, all the "pieces on the board"—the players on your teams—will be more effective...and you'll have more people in the game!

As you seek to be strategic and spiritually sensitive in developing your missional game plan, "calendar" ministry, be intentional about developing *attractional*, *incarnational* and *invitational* ministry. A key is to be sensitive to "receptive" and aware of the "resistant" times on the calendar of people's lives. There are several approaches to keep in mind.

"Church" Calendar

The spiritual holidays of Christmas and Easter are still two times of the year when many unchurched people are open to coming to "church." More liturgical churches are very conscious of the Christian calendar, while other churches virtually ignore it. Whether people are unchurched or dechurched, the realities of Christ's incarnation, crucifixion and resurrection highlight the distinct uniqueness of Jesus as Lord. Planning ministries inside and outside your church during these receptive seasons of the "church" calendar can reap great harvest results.

"Culture" Calendar

Secular special days can also be great times to be intentional about redemptively connecting to people. Many churches are leveraging these days to serve people in ways that meet felt needs.

Consider Super Bowl Sunday, Valentine's Day, St. Patrick's Day, Mother's Day, Father's Day, July 4th, Canada Day, Halloween and Thanksgiving as spiritual harvest opportunities. If you live in another country, what are your special cultural celebrations?

"Community" Calendar

Every community has special events that provide ways for churches to become known as valuable servants and community partners. Community festivals during seasons are times to implement the principle *"where people congregate, we will operate."* The schedules of area schools, city park and recreation departments, business events and hunting/fishing seasons are all part of the "community calendar." All provide ways for churches to be seen as an important part of community life. Serving in these ways develops relationships and continues nurturing receptivity among sphere of *"Where people congregate, we will operate."* influence leaders. Churches don't always have to plan events to get people to come to them, we can go where people already are and demonstrate God's love in practical ways there!

"Celebration/Crisis" Calendar

People are more spiritually accessible in times of transition in their lives. Pay attention to birth, marriage or death announcements, those going through divorce or grief, people who have recently moved or people dealing with addiction. Churches that sensitively reach out and develop ministries to meet those needs will often find receptive people.

"Circumstance" Calendar

Occasionally special things happen that are not on any of the other calendars we've mentioned. For example, the events of 9-11 were a circumstance where many people sought hope, truth and comfort. A weather related disaster or a families dislocated by fire or flood can be a powerful way for a church to serve others in loving, tangible ways. In a different vein, many churches leveraged the release of movies with spiritual themes as a great way to redemptively engage their communities. There may be other opportunities for churches to team up for special events in their area. It's a powerful witness to people outside the church to see different churches working together as God's team! Churches need to be ready to mobilize their efforts quickly to make the most of these circumstances for bringing Good News to people.

If you are planting a church, be especially sensitive and intentional about launching your regular Sunday gatherings in a receptive season of your community's calendar. Often this is in the springtime leading up to Easter and in the fall as school begins, but pay attention to the unique dynamics of your local mission field.

How intentional are you about developing a "missional calendar"? When we are spiritually sensitive and also strategic in our efforts, we will see great harvest results. You can be intentional, incarnational and invitational in your ministry!

Discern Missional Partners

Studying your mission field redemptively and finding receptive "S*o*I*L" often leads to great missional partnerships! When you partner with a group or organization in your community, you don't always have to create or manage the program. Instead, you can just invest time and energy directly into serving people. You don't have to develop a new ministry. You can join someone else in their environment in a way that produces a win/win outcome.

When you simply join another group in a missional partnership, two networks of relationships are created: relationships with those we serve and those we serve with. Missional partnerships also include the people you take with you to serve. There are many unchurched people who are very receptive to participating in community service projects before they might be open to attending church.

Who is Jesus calling you to serve with? There are many possibilities—community organizations, social service agencies, local schools, local businesses, nonprofits, other churches—every community has opportunities for missional partnerships. Who you choose to partner with is determined by a number of factors, including their receptivity, policies, the relational connections you have with them and the "OK" of the Holy Spirit. There are some organizations you may not feel comfortable with because of priorities or values. However, remember that the Lord is sending you to be Good News to the people you serve with, not just the people you serve! Wisely discern where you can find *common ground for the common good* and experience *common grace* as you develop missional partners. *Common grace* can become *converting grace*.

Another group to consider might be the unchurched people you know who are interested in serving. People are often looking for a cause bigger than themselves that makes a difference. As the people of your church talk about what they are doing out in the community with their friends, family, neighbors and coworkers, you will find interest and receptiveness in unexpected and rewarding ways! Sometimes a short-term mission trip to another country can be a great opportunity. Pray about who you could invite to serve with you...then ask! An invitation to serve together can become bridges to salvation.

Think of those your church serves as potential ministry partners. As we serve, love, listen and pray intentionally, we will gain favor and build relationships with people. The Lord supernaturally connects who we are as God's Kingdom Team to those in our mission field who are receptive to Him. Although the Good News is for everyone, you will discern those with whom the Lord has given you favor, affinity and relationship. These people can be described as a "Ministry Focus Group" (MFG). Spiritual sensitivity leads to strategic ministry to those the Lord's been preparing for us to reach!

Who are the people that the Lord is giving you favor, affinity and relationship with? These become your Ministry Focus Group... your "MFG."

Blend together the insights from your intercession, intentional study, serving opportunities and God's divine appointments. Include people with whom you discover you share common interests and free time, values and beliefs, vocational issues or personal or community needs. Describe what your MFG looks like.

Develop Missional Bridges

Ministry activities require effort to become missional bridges. Always plan how you will leverage an activity to build bridges to Jesus and into your church. *Plan each event with the next one in mind.* The more bridges we build for people, the more who will cross over into life in Christ, fruitful relationships with others and meaningful ministry. A ministry out in the community should bridge to one at your church.

Here are some ways to create "missional bridges":

"Taste and See" Plan small and large group opportunities for people to get to know you and your church's vision, values and mission. Let them "taste and see that the Lord is good...and our church is too!"

"Go and Serve" Go out (sometimes partnering with other community groups) to serve redemptively, demonstrating God's love in practical ways. This is where to deploy your ministry and mission teams. Remember, "Where people congregate, we will operate."

"Learn and Grow" Develop short term seminars or groups to meet felt needs, usually four- to six-weeks long. These groups can meet inside or outside your church.

"Get to Know" Develop creative ways for people to connect relationally. "Social" can be "spiritual" too! People want to experience life in community. As we do life together, we can see grace at work in each other.

These strategies do not need to be done sequentially. It's more important that they be done sensitively in order to leverage them for building ministry momentum. The key is always being intentional about the relationships they make possible.

As you develop your missional strategy in terms of who you will serve and who you will serve with, give yourself flexibility for "missional discovery." Experiment and field test to see what works and what doesn't. See where the Lord is blessing and join Him. Don't be afraid to change where you devote your missional energy.

COACH YOURSELF FORWARD

1. What insights did you gain from the word picture about "learning to play without the queen"? How can you apply these insights in your leadership conversations and your ministry planning?

2. As you process issues related to developing a missional lifestyle and a missional calendar, what did you discover that helps you shape your missional game plan?

3. What events can we connect with in order to meet people where they already gather? What is on our community's calendar that should be seen as an opportunity to serve? Remember, "Where people congregate, we will operate."

4. What are your options in regard to missional partners in your community? God's partners may be surprising, so give Him room to work in the relationships He gives you.

5. How will you equip others to invite their unchurched friends to join you in serving your community?

6. What creative ways can you think of "missional bridges" connecting others with God through ministry activities in and outside your church?

7. How will you be intentional about building momentum and connecting what you are doing outside the church with ministries inside the church? Remember, always think about how to leverage an event forward to the next events or redemptive opportunities.

FURTHER RESOURCES

Tangible Kingdom, Hugh Halter and Matt Smay. Jossey-Bass, 2008.

Tangible Kingdom Primer (for small groups), Hugh Halter and Matt Smay. Missio Publishing, 2009.

Conspiracy of Kindness, Steve Sjogren. Regal, 2008.

101 Ways to Reach Your Community, Steve Sjogren. NavPress, 2000.

101 Ways to Help People in Need, Steve and Janie Sjogren. NavPress, 2002.

5 Things Any Congregation Can Do to Care for Others, Jason Cusick. WPH, 2009.

Mobilizing for Compassion: Moving People into Ministry, Robert Logan and Larry Short. Fleming H. Revell, 2004.

Heartbeat: How to Turn Passion into Ministry, Chip Arn. Xulon Press, 2011.

Missional Communities: The Rise of the Post-Congregational Church, Reggie McNeal. Jossey-Bass, 2011.

Exiles: Living Missionally in a Post-Christian Culture, Michael Frost. Hendrickson Publishers, 2006.

The Art of Neighboring: Building Genuine Relationships Right Outside Your Door, Jay Pathak and Dave Runyon. Baker Books, 2012.

Appendix C
"Developing a Missional Calendar"
"Living Sent: Developing a Missional Lifestyle"
"Developing Missional Bridges"

"Storytelling"
That Makes Good News Real

Over the next several weeks, Tom and Bill worked together with church leaders to implement the game plan in their community. Although some struggled with and resisted the focus on reaching lost people and doing ministry out in the community, many others were energized and engaged. People who had been mostly inactive now found fresh ways to be included. The stories of what the Lord was doing through their service became a wonderful buzz throughout the church. "Living sent" and "being a missionary" were more than catch phrases for people...they were daily reality! Ideas for new ministries and teams arose from the discoveries and relationships they made.

"It's happening!" exclaimed Tom as they got together for their coaching visit. "I feel like I'm becoming the missionary and missional leader I've longed to become. We talk about influencing people for Jesus 'every day in every way' all the time. I've had the privilege of bringing some of my neighbors to Christ. Some of them are beginning to come to our worship services."

"That's awesome!" exclaimed Bill. "Nothing fuels my heart like seeing someone find life in Christ. I can see it in your eyes, too! How are things going overall as a church?"

"We're on a real learning curve," replied Tom. "Some things we tried didn't work out as we had hoped, but other doors are opening to us in supernatural ways. We're having opportunities to love and serve people in ways we'd prayed could happen... now it is! It's also been very humbling. At first we tended to approach our service as things we were doing *for* people. But we found ourselves learning so much *from* the people we were serving. The Lord's been changing our attitudes. Now we are doing life *with* people instead of doing things *for* people. We're hearing their stories and finding ways to share our own stories in such natural ways. We're enjoying new relationships and friendships...God's giving us increasing favor out in our community. Since we've become more intentional about building bridges into our mission field, it's making it so much easier to invite people back over those bridges to things we're doing in our building.

The two men gave each other a fist bump in celebration. "Way to go, God!" exclaimed Bill. "How's it been going for your ministry buddies? I know you've been learning to coach each other as you all develop your own missional game plans. What are you learning from them?"

"As I've debriefed with my friends around the country and the world, they have all personalized their own unique game plan. Yet, we are finding similar results," said Tom. "One of my friends described what he's experiencing as changing from a professional minister doing church work to a missional leader leading a team of missionaries out into their mission field. We're changed leaders! The process you've been helping me develop through your coaching has been rippling out through their ministries, too."

Bill smiled, "It is amazing how the process just unfolds itself, isn't it? Whether it's growing coaching skills or missional ministry skills, I learned that we tend to follow a progression. First, we're unaware and unable... we don't know what we need to know and we don't know what to do. Next, we become conscious but uncomfortable...we know what we should do, but we struggle to know how to do it. Then we reach the point of being comfortable and increasingly competent...we know what to do and feel like we're getting good at it. The ultimate goal is to become supernaturally natural...we work hard to get good at the skills, but we are conscious that it all flows from the work of the Holy Spirit in and through us. What I heard you describing is how the Lord is empowering you to be supernaturally natural as a missional leader. I can see how much the Lord has grown you. I'll say it again: Way to go, God!"

> **"The Progression of Growing Our Skills"**
> Unaware and unable...
> Conscious but uncomfortable...
> Comfortable and increasingly competent...
> *Supernaturally natural!*

Tom nodded humbly, "Thanks. I'm so grateful for how the Lord has used you to help me grow, too. But, I've still got a long way to go!"

"We all do, brother," replied Bill. "Still, it's important to stop and see how far He's brought us sometimes. So, fellow missionary...what's the goal of our conversation today?"

"We need to work on the *storytelling* part of our missional pathway. Because we've been out making redemptive friendships, we are seeing more people come to our Sunday morning gatherings. We're finding out how true it is that many people are open to come to our worship services if only someone they know and trust would just invite them. That's been thrilling! We've been asking our guests for their feedback about their experience at church and..." Tom paused.

"And? What have you been learning?" asked Bill.

"Well, I think I understand what it is like for you as a missionary even more," said Tom. "We found out that things we take for granted about what we say and how we do "church" can be unfamiliar and even confusing for people who are not used to church. They really want to know Jesus, but sometimes it's like we're speaking a foreign language to them. I want our church to speak their language so we aren't hindering them from coming to Christ!"

Bill nodded, "I've had very similar experiences as a missionary. I had to learn to relate to others on their level and speak their language. When it came to introducing them to worship and the Gospel, we had to learn how to translate the Good News for them instead of making them interpret it for themselves...and there's a big difference. We didn't change the message of the Gospel, but we had to change how we communicated it."

An "aha" look came to Tom's face. "That's what we need to do better!" he exclaimed. "We need to adapt the way we do church with new people in mind. Instead of assuming that everyone knows what's going on, we'll have to be intentional about translating what we're doing so new people can understand and respond to Christ. The only barriers I want people to have to overcome in choosing Christ are the choices they make of their own free will. So, how about if we focus on how we can share God's story better. Let's work on some translation skills!"

Bill laughed. "I love it! I wish more pastors and churches were doing that. I visit so many churches that frankly have not prepared for new people. Sometimes what I see and hear makes me cringe. To hear a pastor like you want to be intentional about translating the Good News is music to my ears. So let's get a picture of where you and your church are when it comes to becoming great storytellers. Who do we need to equip with good storytelling skills? In what ways are you doing a good job right now? In what ways do you need to pay attention to how our church presents ourselves and the Gospel? How can we be better?"

Tom nodded. "Good questions. Let's paint our picture of reality and then generate some options that we turn into our game plan."

Bill grinned. "You've got the GROW coaching plan down well! May I make an observation that might help our conversation further?"

"Sure," Tom said.

Bill continued, "One of the priorities I've learned as a missionary was to be both incarnational and invitational. It wasn't enough for us to **We have to be intentional about being both incarnational *and* invitational to bring Jesus to people and people to Jesus!** just do good things in Jesus' name. We had to be intentional about making sure we shared the plan of salvation clearly and invited people to cross the line of faith and commit their lives to Christ. So, another question for you to consider is, how will you be intentional about being both incarnational *and* invitational to bring people to Jesus?"

"That's a great insight," returned Tom. "My ministry friends and I have been talking about very similar issues. Some of our younger leaders at church have been thrilled by how we are showing Jesus to people incarnationally while some of our older leaders are reminding me that our goal is still to invite people to be saved. Let's make sure we're paying attention to both as we get to our action steps."

Together, Tom and Bill identified a number of areas that needed attention in their ministry. They realized that they needed to equip their people better to share their own story and the plan of salvation in a simple and natural way. They decided that ask some friends to act like "mystery shoppers" when they came to church and get their feedback about how the church could be better prepared for new people. They also determined that they needed to look at how the church described itself through their media and other means.

"We have to address our storytelling and translating in more ways than I would have guessed!" Tom said as he looked at his action steps. "It's how we look, it's what we say, it's what people see and hear and smell, it's being sensitive to all ages and stages of life...we can't take anything for granted."

"True...but you're developing a great game plan to help you improve," said Bill. "We're making great progress...and it's only going to get better for those we want to reach!"

The two leaders laid their game plan before the Lord, praying for His wisdom and favor and inviting Him to lead them. "Let Your Kingdom come...let Your will be done here in us and through us as You've already mapped it out from heaven, Lord. We're here for Your purposes...we're all Yours...lead us according to Your plan!"

Translating His Story in Groups

One effective way of making God's Word accessible to people is called "Discovery Bible Study" or DBS. It is working powerfully in many cultures around the world. It can be used by and even led by people who are new to the Bible. Dependent on the power of God's Word and the Holy Spirit, it forms the basis for "obedience and promise based discipleship." For many people, Bible study and discipleship is more about information—what you know—than transformation—how you live. In order to see transformation, we need to obey the commands of Jesus and rely on the promises of Jesus He gives us in His Word. Here is a simple pattern for leading a small group Discovery Bible Study:

Discovery Bible Study Priorities
1. Start with a Person of Peace (Luke 10:6)
2. Seek to lead a person/family/group to discover God and His salvation. We seek to build obedience-and- promise-based disciples who make disciples who make disciples!
3. The Scripture is the authority. Lead a simple inductive Bible Study each week.
   * Group Interaction

Discovery Bible Study --Connecting Relationally
   *Accountability
   Ask: What are you thankful for this week? (Prayer)
   Ask: What needs do you or others have? (Intercession)

Ask: How can we help meet the needs expressed? (Ministry)
* Bible Study
Ask: With whom did you share last week's lesson? (Evangelism)
Ask: How did you apply what you learned last week? (Obedience)

The Discovery Bible Study Process—Connecting to God's World

1st Pass: Read the Scripture Text
- What did you like most about this passage?
- What did you find difficult or confusing in this passage?

2nd Pass: Read the Passage Again
- What does this passage teach us about God?
- What does this teach us about ourselves?

3rd Pass: Ask someone to retell the story or passage.
- If this is true, how would we have to obey? What does God want you to do about it? What promise do you see about how God will help you obey?
- Who can you share what you just learned with?

For pre-believers you can start with Creation and work through Bible to Christ, focusing on the attributes of God. For new believers you will start with commands of Christ.

Focus on the Scripture, not human opinion...trust the Holy Spirit!

(Adapted from: Discovery Bible Study, David Watson. Get further information at: http://e3partners.org/resources/learning -resources/)

Translating His Story at Church

Christology...missiology...ecclesiology. Sent...Student...Servant... Storyteller. Listening to serving and relating to our mission field shape our style of church and strategy for ministry, which influences how we "tell the Story." As we prayerfully discern in whom God has called us to invest intentionally for Kingdom purposes, we have to learn how to best communicate the Good News to them more effectively.

When people come to church, do we translate for them or do they have to interpret? Think about the last time you went to a "new" place. Perhaps you came at the invitation of a friend or you just wanted to check it out because something there interested you. What was the experience like? How easy was it for you to understand where to go and what to do? How welcome did the people there make you feel? How much did they "translate" things for you so you could understand what was going on? How much did you have to "interpret" without any help? What made you want to go back? What made you not want to go back?

Increasing numbers of people in our culture have little or no church or biblical background. They don't understand church language and practices as we do, so everything is new to them. The key issue for us as we seek to tell the story of Jesus is to make sure we are translating it for them...going out of our way to help them understand, appreciate and enter in so they can meet Jesus at their level. Remember what is familiar to us may be confusing to others. Be concerned about things like...

- **Website and social media**—Before most people ever attend a church, they first check out your website or Facebook page. How clear and understandable is your media? How well are you answering the questions that someone new to your church would ask? Can they easily identify when and where you meet?
- **Verbiage and terms**—No matter whether they are biblical, theological, make sure you translate churchy language for unchurched people!
- **Unfamiliar spaces**—Does your church have hosts and hospitality teams for newcomers to welcome, guide and answer questions? It's been said the new people decide whether they want to come back to a church within the first few minutes...before they even hear its music or listen to a message!
- **Signs and maps**—After people find your address, can they also find restrooms and children's classrooms?
- **Your church's "look" and "smell"**—What do people see and smell? How clean, fresh and inviting are we?
- **Worship style and patterns**--Tell guests what you're doing in your service and why.
- **Names of people and places**—Church people we know by first name ("See Sue for more information" or "We'll meet over at the Smiths'") are unknown to new people!

One thing you can do is to invite someone to be a "secret worshiper" visiting your church with fresh eyes. A "Secret Worshiper Survey" is included in Appendix C.

Here are key questions to ask:

- What redemptive analogy or biblical story best describes how to engage your Ministry Focus Group (MFG)?
- What would be "Good News" to our MFG? What would it look and sound like to them?
- What style of "church" will minister to our MFG most effectively? How can we make sure our church services are designed with new people in mind?
- How can we creatively, consistently and clearly communicate the Good News to our community in order to bring people closer to a saving knowledge of Christ?
- How will we create intentional opportunities to invite people to commit their lives to Christ?

The best compliment we can receive from someone who comes to visit our church is "It was like you were expecting me to come today!"

Telling Your Personal Story

"But in your hearts set apart Christ as Lord. Always be prepared to give an answer to anyone who asks you to give the reason for the hope that you have. But do this with gentleness and respect...." (1 Peter 3:15)

"Devote yourselves to prayer with an alert mind and a thankful heart. Pray for us, too, that God will give us many opportunities to speak about his mysterious plan concerning Christ. That is why I am here in chains. Pray that I will proclaim this message as clearly as I should. Live wisely among those who are not believers and make the most of every opportunity. Let your conversation be gracious and attractive so that you will have the right response for everyone." (Colossian 4:2-6, NLT)

We meet people at different places along a spiritual journey continuum. We've already learned that our first practice should be redemptive listening--the process of hearing their story, sharing your story so we can connect them to His Story! Everyone has a story to tell. The Lord will help you learn to share your story in a natural way that fits who you are. The Holy Spirit will supernaturally use your story to influence others in remarkable ways!

Make sure you take the time to listen to the stories of those you serve. As you do, you'll find the keys to their heart—their longings, wounds, dreams, broken places, dreams and needs. Share the parts of your story that connects to theirs. Find a way to share the Story of Jesus that meets them on a heart level. As Colossian 4:2-6 reminds us, it is a great honor to take the mystery out of knowing God. Here are basic ingredients for blending your story with God's Story so your friends and discover how He connects to their story too.

- Before I met Jesus, my life was….

- I realized I needed Jesus when…..

- I committed my life to Jesus by….

- Since I met Jesus my life is…..

- You can know Jesus, too, by…..

Telling Your Church's Story

It's been often said that word-of-mouth is the most effective form of marketing. The way our missional game plan helps us listen to, relate with and serve others provides practical and natural ways for your church to create "word-of-mouth" opportunities for telling your church's story. Many churches have worked on a mission statement that describes their vision, values and strategy. Often these are only "in-house" documents, which is important. However, it's also important to develop ways to "tell the story" of your church for those you want to invite to Christ and your fellowship. Think about how you can communicate your vision, values and mission in concise, energizing ways for unchurched people.

- *Vision*—paints a positive picture of what God is doing in and through your church for His glory…WHERE He is leading you.

- *Values*—describes your priorities--WHY you do what you do.

- *Mission*—states WHO you want to reach, WHAT their needs are and HOW you are meeting those needs to bring them to Christ.

Remember, your mission field will shape these issues. If you can share your story in an energizing, memorable way in a sentence, you may invite longer conversations that build bridges to people.

Consider how you will "tell your story" on three levels:

- *Coffee cup or T-shirt*—your message in a simple, memorable sentence or phrase.

- *Elevator speech or Tweet*—your story in 10-15 seconds that invites further conversation.

- *Bullet points*—your vision, values and mission in an extended conversation or as you present yourself through your website, blogs, Facebook page or other media.

As we said, personal "word of mouth" conversations are the best, but there are many other means you can use to communicate your church's story. Consider various forms of media that fit best fit in your context: mailings, TV or radio spots, invite cards your people can hand out, billboards, website, social media, blogs, etc. There are many creative and often inexpensive ways to communicate!

The main issue is to make sure you are translating your church's story in ways that are interesting, energizing, inviting and memorable for the people on your mission field. Share your church's story! Share it often, share it well and expect people to respond. Remember, they're waiting for us!

COACH YOURSELF FORWARD

1. When we talked about "translating" for new people, what issues did you identify that need your immediate attention?

2. What can you do to see your church's facilities, ministries, means of communication and services through the eyes of new people? How can you be intentional about that kind of evaluation in order to capture insights you need to address?

3. What action steps do you need to take to make your facilities and ministries more welcoming and understandable for new people?

4. How are you developing ways to include and connect new people to your church?

5. In what ways could you better equip the people of your church to share their story and God's Story in simple, clear and natural ways?

6. How are you sharing your church's story with your community? In what ways can you be more clear, energizing and memorable?

7. Consider the many methods and means you can use to share your church's story. What are you currently doing? What are some new possibilities? How will you integrate them?

FURTHER RESOURCES

Perfect Blend DVD and group study, Chris Conrad. WPH, 2009.

Five Things Anyone Can Do to Introduce Someone to Jesus, Chris Conrad. WPH, 2007.

Missing in America, Tom Clegg. Group Publishing, 2007.

Five Things Anyone Can Do to Help Their Church Grow, Phil Stevenson. WPH, 2007.

Becoming a Contagious Christian, Bill Hybels and Mark Mittleburg. Zondervan, 1996.

Knowing God booklet, Keith Drury. WPH, 2006.

The Real Purpose of Life booklet, "Real Purpose of Life" P.O. Box 814, Milwaukee, WI 53201

http://e3partners.org/resources/learning-resources/

Appendix C
"Listening to their Story and Sharing Yours"
"Discovery Bible Study"
"Secret Worshiper Survey"

"Spreading"
Grace to New Places

"Bill, tell me again how you and your team planted churches in so many places," said Tom at their next coaching visit.

"I'd be glad to, but why do you ask?" replied Bill.

"The Lord's been stirring some new things in us as a team," said Tom. "We've been living out our missional game plan as a church and God's been doing wonderful things in us and through us. You know what we've been doing out in our mission field. We've started a new service to help us reach more people right in our own building. We're a different church now! It's been more difficult and yet rewarding than we could have dreamed. Like the old Army slogan, missional ministry is "the toughest job you'll ever love!" It's been the greatest adventure in my leadership journey. As grateful as we are, we believe the Lord is calling us beyond our church to do more."

"In what ways has the Lord been speaking to you?" Bill asked, intense interest on his face.

"He's speaking to us in several ways. He's increasing our hunger for more people to come to know Him. As people come to Christ, we find ourselves pleading with the Lord to trust us with even more souls. I find myself praying for our community like one of my ministry heroes, John Knox, used to pray for his nation, 'Give me Scotland or I'll die!' The Lord's also stretching the way we see our mission field. There are some people who probably don't feel like our church is the best fit for them. What if we could start a ministry or new site or a new church that was designed for them? There are people who are now coming to our church who drive from a distance. It's hard for them to invite their neighbors to come so far. What if we started a church for them where they live? What if we could invest more intentionally in starting churches in places far from us, like the mission field you serve? We're starting to understand what John Wesley meant when he said, 'The world is my parish.'"

"That's great, Tom!" Bill exclaimed, his face shining. "I've been praying for the Lord to expand your boundaries and increase your influence for Him. He's moving you toward multiplication ministry with an Acts 1:8 mindset."

"What do you mean by an Acts 1:8 mindset?" asked Tom.

"It's a simple way to discern potential mission fields," said Bill. "When Jesus said He would send the Holy Spirit to give us supernatural power to be His witnesses, He identified four places that help us. Remember what they are?"

"Jerusalem, Judea, Samaria and the ends of the earth," responded Tom. "What might that mean for us today?"

"Great question," said Bill. Grabbing a sheet of paper, he wrote:

- Jerusalem: people **like** us and **near** us

- Judea: people **like** us but **not near** us

- Samaria: people **not like** us but **near** us

- Ends of the earth: people **not like us** and **not near us**

"Now with that view of Acts 1:8 in mind, how does that relate to what the Lord's been saying to you?" asked Bill.

"Wow…it fits perfectly!" exclaimed Tom. "That will really help us think about the potential scope of our missional ministry from a biblical but simple perspective. If the Lord is calling us to take His grace to new places, how can we do that? How could we use the principles that helped us design our game plan to do missional ministry in other places?"

"Is that what you want to focus on today?"

"Is that a rhetorical question?" teased Tom. "Let's go after it and see how we can do what the Lord's been saying to us!"

Together Tom and Bill adapted the same missional pathway they had followed for Tom's church and coached themselves to a game plan that would equip their church to multiply their ministry in new ways and settings.

It wouldn't be the last time Tom coached his leaders through a similar process.

"Who"—Looking with an Acts 1:8 Mindset

"But you will receive power when the Holy Spirit comes upon you and you will be My witnesses in Jerusalem, in all Judea and Samaria and to the ends of the earth." (Acts 1:8)

An Acts 1:8 perspective allows us to engage in maximum missional ministry! Beyond our initial Ministry Focus Group (see

"Jerusalem"), the Lord wants us to pay attention to other opportunities He's preparing. Using Acts 1:8 as a missional grid, prayerfully consider new possibilities to spread grace to new places. Who are the people your local church has the greatest potential to impact for Christ?

Jerusalem—People **near** us and **like** us. They will come to Christ and our worship gatherings as we will find ways to build redemptive bridges to them.

Judea—People **like** us, but not **near** us. They would come to our worship gatherings, but are too far away. What kinds of ministries or another church could we start to reach them where they live?

Samaria—People **near** us, but not **like** us. They may not connect easily to our church, but we could start another ministry, service or church for them even though it's close to our own church. What people groups or special opportunities might fit "Samaria" ministry?

Ends of the earth—People not **like** us and not **near** us. Increasingly, ministry is blending local and global to become "glocal." Consider how you can partner with missionaries in other parts of the world to plant churches and other missional initiatives. Work with your denomination's global mission team to discover what opportunities might fit your church.

"Where"—Following the Spirit's Lead

Discerning where the Lord might have your church launch a new initiative takes prayer and strategic wisdom. With your leaders, consider these questions:

- Who is the Lord giving us a burden for?

- Who is a person of peace that could give us access to more people?

- Where is the Lord giving us favor and open doors?

Sometimes we may have a desire to go in a particular direction but have the Lord restrain or redirect us. Acts 16:4-10 prompts us to ask, "Where might the Lord be giving us an unexpected "Macedonian call"?

Then they went from town to town, instructing the believers to follow the decisions made by the apostles and elders in Jerusalem.[5] So the churches were strengthened in their faith and grew larger every day. Next Paul and Silas traveled through the area of Phrygia and Galatia, because the Holy Spirit had prevented them from preaching the word in the province of Asia at that time. Then coming to the borders of Mysia, they headed north for the province of Bithynia, but again the Spirit of Jesus did not allow them to go there. So instead, they went on through Mysia to the seaport of Troas. That night Paul had a vision: A man from Macedonia in northern Greece was standing there, pleading with him, "Come over to Macedonia and help us!" So we decided to leave for Macedonia at once, having concluded that God was calling us to preach the Good News there. (Acts 16:4-10 NLT)

- Where are clusters of people from our church living that might indicate a new ministry location or initiative? Where are clusters of people who might speak a different language or come from a different culture where we could develop redemptive relationships and ministry?

- What invitations have we received from our missional partners?

- Who has the Lord brought to our church that could become a missionary to lead a new initiative?

- What are we hearing from our leaders? Pay special attention to what the Lord is birthing in their hearts!

- How could we join the bigger team of churches in our district, denomination or mission agency as a partner?

"When"—Timing and Timelines

As you do the work of spiritual discernment, you'll also need to do the work of strategic planning. Designing a ministry flow chart and timeline will help you organize and optimize new ministry designs.

A ministry flow chart is a diagram of major ministries, programs, teams and events.

- It shows each ministry in relation to the others.

- It shows the logical sequence by which people become connected and involved step by step.

- It shows the intended result of ministry involvement.

- It is useful to show what ministries might be missing, especially missional teams.

- It shows how your missional game plan begins out in your mission field, makes disciples and then deploys disciples and teams back into your mission field!

- It has missional multiplication in mind!

Here's an exercise for evaluating and expanding your church's current ministries. List each major ministry team, event or program that you currently have or plan to have on a Post-it® note. If you are starting a new service, ministry or church, plan with your intended outcome in mind.

Organize the Post-it® notes in a pathway on a poster board to show how you will connect to unchurched people, lead them to Christ, grow them in leadership and equip them as a reproducing leader. Make sure you can see an intentional disciple-making pathway.

If designing a new ministry (or church), put dates on the pathway so it also becomes a timeline. Although you are more "checkpoint" than calendar driven in your planning, set a date in the future for the new ministry to begin and work backward from this launch date to establish the sequence necessary for a successful launch.

Review your work as a team. Identify any missing essential ministries, teams or events. Add them in.

Identify any unnecessary ministry activities and set them aside. Look for "bottlenecks and disconnects"—points where progress can easily be interrupted or hindered. Think about what level of commitment required to be involved at each ministry step. What additional strategies might be needed to grow and equip people at each step? What communication and relationships are needed to move people from one level of commitment and involvement to another?

Now connect the Post-it® notes with arrows to form a pathway and timeline for your game plan. Give yourself permission to adapt your plan as situations warrant. Put everything at the disposal and direction of the Holy Spirit. Dream big. Work hard. Stay dependent. Pray much. Expect! Developing a game plan for missional ministry is one of the most rewarding things you can do…cover everything with prayer, keep at it…and watch God work through you!

For a video that describes the difference between a Ministry Flow Chart and how to develop the "Ministry Timeline" process, go to https://www.youtube.com/watch?v=t_elEXoFW7o. You'll need to develop a ministry flow chart and timeline that describes your unique missional game plan.

COACH YOURSELF FORWARD

1. Review your mission field from an Acts 1:8 perspective. What possibilities can you discover?

2. In what ways is the Lord calling you to spread grace to new places and people?

3. Prayerfully review the questions related to discerning new places for ministry. What further questions could you add? What is the Lord making clear to you?

4. Step back and take a look at your church's "Ministry Flow Chart." What issues might you need to address, especially where there are gaps that hinder the flow of ministry?

5. What area is most important to address first?

6. What new initiative is the Lord calling you to pursue? Design a timeline with the launch of the new ministry or church in mind. Work backward from your launch date and develop your ministry flow chart.

7. How big is your mission field now?

FURTHER RESOURCES

Movements That Change the World, Steve Addison. IVP Books, 2011.

Planting a Missional Church, Ed Stetzer. B&H Academic, 2006.

Five Things Anyone Can Do to Start a Church, Phil Stevenson. WPH, 2008.

There are many great e-books and resources at:
www.exponential.org/resources/

Appendix C
"Acts 1:8 Strategy"
"Ministry Flowchart and Timeline"

Afterword

The time came for Bill and his family to head back to their ministry assignment overseas. Tom and Bill got together over coffee one last time at their usual place to reflect on what the Lord had done over the months that they walked together. As they did, they gave the thanks and glory to the Lord for all He had done.

"What began as an invitation to coffee and conversation became a life changing coaching relationship for me," said Tom. "I had a longing to bring Jesus to our community so people could know how much He loves them. The missional game plan that came out of our coaching relationship changed the course of my own life, our church and our influence in our community. Now Jesus is famous in so many more ways. So many have come home to the Father! It's not uncommon for me to hear, 'If your church wasn't here, it would be a huge loss to our community.'"

Bill smiled and nodded, "I can't tell you how grateful I am for what God's doing in my own home town and home church. It's been an honor to walk with you. We can't meet like this for coffee anymore, but we can still stay connected. I'm glad we live in a day where missionaries have email and Skype!"

Tom agreed, "Let's still plan to visit by Skype. I'll need your coaching from time to time. And I'll see you when we bring a short-term team to work with you on your mission field!"

"Can't wait," grinned Bill. "I may not be your coach in the same way, but now we're friends and fellow missionaries."

"Yup...I'm not just a pastor anymore!" laughed Tom. "And I have you to thank for that."

"We both have Him to thank for that and so much more," replied Bill. "Let's tell Him so."

They did.

Bill returned to his mission field. He had continued to coach leaders there even while he was back in the States and their ministries continued to grow in his absence. They continued to multiply more disciples, leaders and churches and they even began sending missionaries to other nations.

Tom went for more training and grew skills for equipping other leaders as a coach. Coaching became a primary way he approached ministry leadership in his church. He now coaches leaders all around the country, seeking to bless them as Bill had blessed him.

Tom's ministry buddies around the country and the world found that the principles of developing a missional game plan can be applied in many settings. Their game plans made a huge difference in their own ministries. As they shared the principles with their network of friends, there was a wonderful ripple effect. Many other new ministries and churches were birthed. The dream of ministries that multiplied disciples, leaders, ministries and churches became reality.

A Personal Challenge

It's our dream that these kinds of coaching conversations like you saw with Bill and Tom will take place all the time among all kinds of leaders. As we equip one another with a missional A*C*T*S plan that assesses, coaches, trains both spiritually and strategically, we believe that every church can follow the leading of the Holy Spirit and develop its own game plan for intentional missional ministry. Church planting teams will make a missional game plan an integral part of their ministry strategy. Only then will our vision to "follow the Great Commandment and fulfill the Great Commission" thrive and flourish. We'll make our contribution to Kingdom work in our generation...and raise up the next generation of leaders to make Kingdom history in theirs.

John Wesley's words still summon us across the centuries... *"You have nothing to do but save souls..."*

Let's make our response, *"Everything we do will be about saving souls!"*

Appendix A
Coaching Guideline

Coach_____ Leader_____ Date_____

Remember the Seven Habits of a Great Coach—Listen, Care, Celebrate, Strategize, Train, Disciple, Challenge

As you open—<u>Listen…Care…Celebrate</u>—Personal and Ministry updates

<u>Where is God working?</u> (Clarify Calling, Cultivate Character, Create Community, Connect to Culture)

Goal—(What is the purpose of our visit?) What are we going to <u>focus</u> on today? What <u>result</u> would you like to get from our visit today?

Reality—(Paint a picture of what's really happening) What's really going on? Where is God at work? What's working? What's not? In what ways have you addressed this issue? What have you been learning? What other information do we need to know that will help us address this issue?

<u>"Great Commandment Listening"</u> (from Matthew 22:37-39) Listen for what is going on in the:
- <u>"heart"</u> (spirit)—What have you been hearing from the Lord? What does your heart say?
- <u>"soul"</u> (emotions)—What have you been feeling about this?
- <u>"mind"</u> (reason)—What are the facts? What is the most reasonable way to look at this?
- <u>"strength"</u> (physical)—How is your health? How much time, energy and resources will you need?
- <u>"others as yourself"</u> (other's views)—What would your spouse say about this? Other leaders and friends? If they were in your shoes, what would they say?

Options—(What are our possibilities) Develop a list of ideas. Challenge obstacles by asking, "What if we overcame that?" Keep asking, "What else?" "In what ways could we…"

Will—*(What will you do? What action steps will you take? What is your game plan?) Set "S*M*A*R*T goals—Specific, Measurable, Achievable, Relevant, Time-bound*
- What do you choose to do?
- Where does this fit into the big picture, our master plan?
- When will you begin?
- When will you complete this?
- Who else needs to know?
- Who else will you need? (Think about God's team)
- What resources will be required?
- What other issues do we need to consider in our plan?

Wrapping up...
- What was most helpful to you from our visit today?
- When will we have our next coaching visit?
- Let's pray!

Appendix B
Scriptural Insights for Missional Ministry

Joshua: God's Plan for His People to Take His Promised Land

The mission: acquire and dwell in the land God promised His people. The plan: designed by the Lord, implemented by His leaders as they deployed God's tribes. Military leaders still use the book of Numbers to train soldiers today. The plan had to be adapted to different settings and changing scenarios.

- Every new ministry and church begins in the heart of God.
- God's promises become reality as the Spirit of God leads His people and they follow in obedient faith!

1. God Calls a Leader to Take His People Into "The Land." (1:1-10)

- Joshua was mentored by Moses. Young leaders need this ministry!
- God wants to first reveal Himself to the leader before He reveals His call. God's mandate is undergirded by His promises. The call flows from God's character being developed in the heart of the leader.
- God's leader must be a man of the Word! He must learn to live "promise to promise," not "problem to problem." The attitude of the leader makes all the difference.

2. God Compliments His Call By Confirmation From Others. (1:11-18)

- God calls a "Ministry Team" to support and follow the leader. No vision can be accomplished alone.
- Different people will have differing roles in fulfilling the vision, but all are important.

3. Concentrate on "The Land"—Do Spiritual "Recon." (2:1-24)

- Get to know people in the land—they know their area best!
- See through God's eyes...find the "redemptive gifts" of the land and also the spiritual strongholds.
- Thank God for the "first fruits" of your ministry. "Rahabs" are waiting for you to come!

4. **Complete Consecration Brings Cleansing So We Can Fulfill the Call. (3:1-13; 5:1-12)**
   - Pure hearts allow God to show His power.
   - When "you've never been this way before," complete dependence on God is vital.

5. **Confirming Signs—God's Visible Affirmation of His Call! (3:14-4:24)**
   - God presents a challenge—"a flooded Jordan"—and asks us to step out in obedient faith.
   - Our obstacles become God's opportunities!
   - God's first "confirming signs" to the leader and the people become an exciting part of their future "faith story."

6. **Commence by Addressing Strategic Strongholds. (5:13-27)**
   - Focus on worship before warfare. Strategic intercession is essential!
   - Get a fresh revelation of Jesus. Continually yield to His Lordship...do what He's blessing!
   - Even if God's leading appears "foolish," obey and watch God bring down the walls!

7. **Courageously Deal with "Sin in the Camp." (7:1-26)**
   - Overconfidence from past victories can breed prayerlessness.
   - Hidden sin in a leader's life affects the spiritual climate of the entire group.
   - Spiritual defeat can bring discouragement and doubt.
   - Joshua struggled with "the death of the dream." Most every leader reaches a similar point.
   - God will often allow the dream to "die" so He can resurrect it purified!
   - Spiritual leaders must be willing to deal decisively with sinful conduct.
   - Don't be afraid to lose some people to keep the dream pure. Never compromise eternal values for the sake of temporary expediencies.

8. **Commit Again to Covenant Priorities After Difficult Circumstances. (8:1-29)**
   - Make prayer a top priority again!
   - Get back to following God's plans.
   - Corporately restate the call and reinforce the primacy of God's Word.

9. **Careful! Beware of Deception. (9:1-27)**
   - Lack of prayer = lack of discernment. Satan can be very subtle in diverting our attention.
   - Seek good counsel from others before making major decisions.
   - Allowing ourselves to be deceived damages God's work.

10. **Challenge Demonic Coalitions. (10:1-12:24)**
    - Satan will sometimes come at you with a full scale frontal attack, seeking to overwhelm you.
    - Dedicate the situation to God. Go to God first....pray! PRAY!
    - Dare to try something different at God's direction. He often tailors His strategy to your specific situation.
    - Do what you can do, then expect divine help.
    - Deal thoroughly with enemies...allow no demonized issues to remain.

11. **Conquer "The Land" Geographically and Strategically. (13:1-14:5)**
    - "See" the land as a divine inheritance! God has given it to you to extend His Kingdom!
    - Divide the land geographically.
    - Reduce it into manageable areas.
    - Assign leaders to care for each area.
    - Delegate authority.
    - Divide and conquer.
    - Don't try to take the land all at once.
    - Take good care of spiritual leaders.

12. **Cherish and Nourish Pioneers and Faith-full leaders. (14:6-15)**
    - Praise God for "Calebs!" They are far too rare. If God brings them, give them "mountains" to conquer!
    - Honor visionaries and warriors.
    - Respect women's requests and allow them to lead. (15:17-19; 17:34)

13. **Consistency and Faithfulness--the Keys to Long-Term Ministry. (16-22)**
    - You won't win everyone, but stay faithful to the task. (16:10; 17:12-17; 18:1-10)
    - Challenge people to keep taking ground for God. (17:12-17)
    - Always have "safe places"—cities of refuge. (20:1ff)
    - Keep looking to God and praising Him. (21:43-45)
    - Bless those who have served well. (22:1-6)

14. **Conflict Resolution—Vital to Effective Leadership. (22:10-34)**
    - Most conflict comes from misconceptions and miscommunication more than bad motives.
    - Don't assume and accuse—get the facts first! (22:11-20)
    - Get both sides of the story. (22:21-28)
    - Be willing to change your opinion. (22:30-34)
    - Keep the vision a central priority, not personalities.
    - Healthy conflict resolution usually brings stronger relationships.

15. **Carrying On--Transfer Ownership of the Call and the Vision (23-24)**
    - Remember, rejoice in and refocus on God—His call and His accomplishments.
    - Reissue the call and reconfirm the vision.
    - Renew covenant commitments.
    - Revere Godly leaders...heroes of the faith deserve our respect and honor.

Acts: God's Multiplication Manual

Apostles and disciples of the early Church were the first to live out the Great Commission strategy with the supernatural anointing and authority of the Holy Spirit. The combination of sanctified love from a pure heart, spiritual authority to defeat Satan's strategies and supernatural power for miracles made biblical multiplication an amazing reality. In Acts we can see the principles that made such multiplication possible.

1. **"A Rushing Mighty Wind….the POWER for Multiplication"**
   - The Holy Spirit's purity and power—the essential for ministry (1:8-2:4)
   - The Resurrected Jesus—the Risen Lord IN and THROUGH His people (Acts 4:13)

2. **"The Building was Shaken…PRAYER and Multiplication"**
   - Whatever the need…they went to God first. Prayer was the priority. (Acts 2, 4, 13…)
   - Worship and waiting—dependence on God for everything.
   - Importance of strategic intercession

3. **"Let Your Kingdom Come…the PERSPECTIVE of Multiplication"**
   - A Kingdom perspective—give your best (13:1ff)
   - Kingdom vs. empire. It's not about us building our church as a personal empire, it's about God's team working together to build His Kingdom so He gets all the glory.
   - All churches are involved…this is not only about planting new churches…the focus was expanding the Kingdom through new *and* existing churches.

4. **"To the Ends of the Earth…the PASSION of Multiplication"**
   - From local to global--Jerusalem, Judea, Samaria, to the ends of the earth (Acts 1:8)
   - Divine appointments—letting the Spirit lead to receptive places and people (17:2ff)

5. **"No Other Name...the PRIORITY of Multiplication"**
   - Preach Christ—our intrinsic motivation. This is highlighted twelve times throughout Acts.
   - Unless evangelism is at the core, our efforts may be illegitimate.

6. **"If This is God, You Can't Stop Them...the POSSIBILITIES of Multiplication"**
   - The reality of risk...and importance of persistent, risk taking faith. (Acts 4)
   - The importance of flexibility (Acts 10)

7. **"We Must Obey God Rather Than Men...the PROBLEMS of Multiplication"**
   - Reality, ramifications and reactions. The effect of opposition turned out to be positive at every turn. Use problems as a judo move...use the weight of the opponent against them. (Acts 16)
   - Satanic opposition, religious legalism, struggle over resources and methods, church leadership issues, territorialism, persecution and prison can all be obstacles to multiplication.
   - If the Church did not heed the call to multiply, God allowed persecution.

8. **"I'm Going...Not Knowing What Awaits Me...the PERSEVERANCE of Multiplication"**
   - Many points where the church felt like giving up...their reaction made the difference
   - "Death of a dream"—there are times when God allows our dream to die so we can refocus on the Dream Giver and His plans.
   - "In irons/doldrums"—our disappointments can become God's divine appointments (Acts 16)

9. **"Dedicate...For the Special Work I Have for Them...the PARTNERSHIP of Multiplication"**
   - Leadership development facilitated expansion—Aquila & Priscilla, Apollos, Barnabas, Luke, etc.
   - Gift utilization and empowerment—Acts 6. Phillip and Stephan are examples of allowing others to serve according to their gifts. Later Phillip's daughters served according to their gifts.

- Think T*E*A*M—everyone is a minister, not just the super-stars. We all make vital contributions!

10. **"Come Over and Help Us...the PLACEMENT of Multiplication"**
    - Divine appointments and re-appointments—the Macedonian call, sensitivity to the Spirit (Acts 16)
    - Cultural relevance—Mars Hill (Acts 17), placing our ministry to reach people where they are
    - Keep your eyes on what's going on around you...and allow the Lord to deploy people where He wants them! (Acts 13:1-4)

11. **"It Seems Good to the Holy Spirit and to Us...the PROMOTION of Multiplication"**
    - Leaders can bless or squelch what God is doing. (Acts15)
    - It's not just what we are saying...it's how we say it!
    - Building shared vision is vital for united ministry.
    - Communication takes place on many levels:
        a. Ruling elders to pioneers and young churches (Acts 15)
        b. Peter sharing vision with the community (Acts 2)
        c. Paul and Barnabas—personal (end of Acts 15)
        d. Gospel going to Jerusalem, Samaria and beyond to new people groups.

12. **"Then the Church Grew in Numbers and Enjoyed a Time of Peace...the PLEASURE of Multiplication"**
    - All churches are blessed by multiplication (Acts 9:31)
    - God's pleasure in seeing His Great Commandment and Commission being fulfilled
    - "...proclaiming the Kingdom of God with all boldness and teaching about the Lord Jesus Christ." (Acts 28:30)

..............*and the adventure continues!*
(Bill Malick and Tim Roehl)

Luke 9 and 10: Jesus' Strategy for Reaching New Communities

One of the greatest challenges we face is how to bring Good News to our community and region. Jesus sent His disciples into communities as advance teams for His Kingdom to come. As we watch Jesus send His disciples into ministry, we find His keys for Kingdom ministry...

I. He Sends Us Empowered and Equipped (Luke 9:1-17)

Jesus now called the Twelve and gave them authority and power to deal with all the demons and cure diseases. He commissioned them to preach the news of God's kingdom and heal the sick. He said, "Don't load yourselves up with equipment. Keep it simple; you are the equipment. And no luxury inns—get a modest place and be content there until you leave. If you're not welcomed, leave town. Don't make a scene. Shrug your shoulders and move on." Commissioned, they left. They traveled from town to town telling the latest news of God, the Message and curing people everywhere they went. Herod, the ruler, heard of these goings on and didn't know what to think. There were people saying John had come back from the dead, others that Elijah had appeared, still others that some prophet of long ago had shown up. Herod said, "But I killed John—took off his head. So who is this that I keep hearing about?" Curious, he looked for a chance to see him in action. The apostles returned and reported on what they had done. Jesus took them away, off by themselves, near the town called Bethsaida. But the crowds got wind of it and followed. Jesus graciously welcomed them and talked to them about the kingdom of God. Those who needed healing, he healed.
(vs. 1-10 MSG)

1. He sends us...we have an *apostolic* commission! (9:1, 2) Never forget Who sends us!
2. He empowers us...His provides *abundant ability* ("power") to deal with any situation in both the spiritual and physical *arenas*! (9:1)

3. He *authorizes* us and gives us Kingdom jurisdiction to act in His name when we come! (9:1)
4. He gives us a message to *announce*--the King is here and His Kingdom is come! (9:2)
5. He tells us where to *activate* His power first—meet people's felt and physical needs. (9:2)
6. Our ministry will *attract* some, *antagonize* others and *amaze* others as we show them Jesus. (9:4,5,6,7-17)
7. We must balance intense *activity* with intimate time *alone* with Jesus. (9:10)

II. His Strategy of Evangelism Engagement (10:1-10)

Later the Master selected seventy and sent them ahead of him in pairs to every town and place where he intended to go. He gave them this charge: "What a huge harvest! And how few the harvest hands. So on your knees; ask the God of the Harvest to send harvest hands. "On your way! But be careful—this is hazardous work. You're like lambs in a wolf pack. "Travel light. Comb and toothbrush and no extra luggage. "Don't loiter and make small talk with everyone you meet along the way. "When you enter a home, greet the family, 'Peace.' If your greeting is received, then it's a good place to stay. But if it's not received, take it back and get out. Don't impose yourself. "Stay at one home, taking your meals there, for a worker deserves three square meals. Don't move from house to house, looking for the best cook in town. "When you enter a town and are received, eat what they set before you, heal anyone who is sick and tell them, 'God's kingdom is right on your doorstep!' (MSG)

1. Evangelism always *starts* and is *sustained* with prayer. (10:1,2)
2. We are to be *"street smart"* and keep it *simple*. (10:3,4)
3. *Speak* peace to people with an attitude of blessing. (10:5, 6) Lost people are not our enemy! God wants to express His love to them through us!

4. Fellowship-- *Share* life with them. (10:7, 8) Enter their world.
5. *Seek* to meet their physical needs. Don't be afraid to trust the Lord for His miraculous intervention! (10: 9)
6. *Share* the Good News of God's Kingdom salvation! (10:9, 10) *"God's Kingdom is right on your doorstep!"*

III. Be Sensitive to the Lost!

Here's a "Top Ten List" that describes what the lost are looking for from us as Christians...

10. I don't care how much you know until I know how much you care.
9. Have compassion on me. Don't condemn me because my life's a mess.
8. Ask "permission" to tell me about God; don't just push Him on me. Talk *with* me, not *at* me. Listen to me. Find out about my world before you expect me to be interested in yours.
7. Use words I can understand.
6. Have a sense of humor! I want Christianity that can be enjoyed, not endured.
5. Don't focus on your church. Labels don't mean much to me. I'm looking for people who live like they really love God. Chances are I've been burnt or bored in church situations in the past.
4. Don't just tell me about your faith, show me your faith by serving others in love.
3. Take your time. Don't tell me everything at once. Give me time to let God work in my life.
2. Tell me how God can make a difference in my daily life, not just at church on Sunday. If I'm going to be a Christian, I want it to work in real life.
1. Make Jesus real to me. Show me simply how to know Him from His Word and chances are I'll want to know Him, too. After all, I really do want to go to Heaven.

Appendix C
Game Plan Worksheets

To download these worksheets for use with your team, go to http://timroehl.net/home/game-plan/. You can also contact Tim at TimRoehl@usfamily.net.

Making Missional Shifts

"Missional" means we approach ministry as missionaries...sent by God and blessed by Him to be a blessing to others! Our commission is as old as God's covenant with Abraham in Genesis 12. In our generation it becomes the personal expression of the Great Commandment of Matthew 22:36-40 and the Great Commission of Matthew 28:18-20.

Reggie McNeal, in his book *Missional Renaissance* suggests three major shifts we must make:
1. From inward to outward—focusing on the lost more than the already converted.
2. From doing programs to developing people—focusing on equipping disciples to be disciple-makers.
3. From church to Kingdom—focusing on the big picture of what God is doing, not just our specific church.

In other words, we need to learn to distinguish between missional and attractional approaches to ministry. More and more people in our culture don't know God and aren't familiar with church language and practices. As Colossians 4:2-6 reminds us, it is our responsibility and privilege to take the mystery out of knowing God. It is our responsibility to translate the Good News so others can understand. Missional leaders realize that it should not be the unchurched person's burden to have to interpret what we are saying! *Missional and attractional approaches ministry are both important...not "either/or" but "both/and."* Here's a brief way to compare the two approaches:

Shifts that are affecting missional ministry in our culture...

Generational:	Builder/Boomer	to	Buster/Beginner
Cultural:	Modern	to	Postmodern & Pre-modern
Philosophical:	Organizational	to	Organic/relational
Method:	Attractional	to	Missional/"Missionally Attractive"
Supported:	Fully funded	to	Bi-vocational
Organizational:	Denomination/ District centered	to	Parent/Multi-site
Scope:	Local	to	"Glocal"
Planting Strategy:	Attract a crowd, start a church	to	Engage community... do ministry...start church
Posture:	Apologist	to	Missiologist
	Proclamational	to	Incarnational
	Head first/word	to	Heart first/worship/ experience
Training:	Content centered	to	Context centered

Simply put, our game plan has to be intentionally *incarnational* and *invitational*...not only demonstrating God's love in practical ways, but also intentionally inviting people to make the decision to become a disciple of Jesus.

Shifts We Must Make as Missional Leaders

From...	**To...**
"Losing" people from our church	Sending people on God's mission
Giving up our resources	Investing God's provisions
We're too weak	We have authority through Jesus
We can't afford this	We can't afford not to!
One bigger church	More churches reaching more people
Church is for Christians	Ministry for pre-Christians

From...	To...
Ministry for me	I'm a minister for others
Splitting/dividing	Multiplying/expanding
Programs/preferences	Mission-focused ministries meeting needs
My church first	Jesus' mission as our primary passion
Escape or entertain culture	Engage culture
"Come in here"	"Go out there"
"Come...listen"	"Sent...serving"
Head first	Heart first
Program/institutional	Personal/relational
Start churches/do ministry	Do ministry/start churches
Proclamational	Incarnational and invitational
Believer-focused	Harvest-focused
Church-centered	Community-based
Wesley's theology	Wesley's theology *and* methods
"Believe...then you can belong"	"Belong...and you'll want to believe"

COACH YOURSELF FORWARD

1. When you look at the words "Christology, Missiology, Ecclesiology," what order would best describe your current personal priorities?
2. What order would best describe your church's current priorities?
3. What issues need to be addressed in order to have your life and ministry aligned with God's missional priorities?
4. What insights did you gain from the different biblical passages we highlighted? (See Appendix B)
5. How can you begin to apply those insights to your present ministry?
6. What shifts do you need to make in order to be more intentionally missional?
7. What are your next steps to make those shifts?

"Leverage Your Life"
Discovering Ways to Make a Difference for God in Your Daily Life
II Corinthians 5:14-21

Pay Attention...Discern Where God's at Work

1. What do you *enjoy* that could be leveraged redemptively

2. What energizes you? Interests, hobbies, skills...

3. What *experiences* have you had that the Lord could leverage redemptively?

4. What existing *environments* could you leverage more intentionally for redemptive relationships?
   - Work
   - Friendships/relationships
   - Kids' activities (if it applies)
   - Neighbors
   - Other activities

5. What "divine *encouragements*" do you sense from the Lord to be used by Him...both inside and outside the church?
   - What burdens you?
   - What are you passionate about?
   - What desires do you have to be used by the Lord?
   - What sense of calling do you have?
   - What doors of opportunity do you see?

Practical Application...Deploy Daily as God's Missionary!
Coach Yourself Forward

1. As you prayed through how you can leverage your life—through what you enjoy, experiences you've had, environments you live in and divine encouragements from the Lord-- what has the Lord called to your attention?

2. How can you be more specific and intentional where the Lord is leading you? Who...where...when...how? Develop at least two specific and doable action steps you can implement in the next two weeks.

3. Who can you have join you in prayer? Who can check in with you for healthy accountability as you leverage your life as God's missionary?

Discerning Your Ministry Contribution

Key verses: Psalm 32:8; Romans 12:1-3; Philippians 2:13

Key question: *"When do I most often experience God's power, joy and fruit in my life?"*

1. The people and circumstances that have most shaped my life are...

2. The qualities of character I most want God to shape into my own life are _____ _____. Why?

3. People who know me well believe I am most used by God when I am involved in _____ _____. Why?

4. My daily activities that contribute most to God's kingdom are _____ _____. Why?

5. When I think about making a difference for God, I would love to focus more on_____ _____. Why?

6. Though I may have dismissed the thought many times for various reasons, I sometimes feel I really should be doing_____
_____. Why?

7. When people talk about a passion for ministry, I often begin to think about giving my life to accomplishing_____
_____. Why?

Personal vision calls for discerning the
influences that have created a passion
for God and a passion to accomplish
something special for His kingdom.
What insights or themes surfaced in my reflections?

Spheres of Intercessors

Developing a prayer team that protects spiritual leaders is often dramatically undervalued. A good model to follow is Jesus' 3-12-70 -120 expanding spheres of people. What could your teams of intercessors look like?

- **Your "Inner Circle"**—those who know you best, have the gift of intercession and are called to pray for you. You can tell them everything...your deepest needs and issues. The Inner Circle is typically three to five people. Communicate with them often...and consider them always "on call" for prayer no matter what time of day or night. Who are those in your "Inner Circle"?

- **Your "Twelve"**—people who know you well and you trust to pray often for you. You can share with them almost every-thing...they will pray for you more than the project. These people need to be informed regularly. Who are your "Twelve"?

- **Your "Extended Community"**—these are people who know you and will occasionally pray for you. They will be interested in general information and requests about your ministry. You will probably communicate with them every one to three months. Who should be on this list?

One of the essential priorities for leaders is to keep their intercessors informed, active and involved. What do you share with your prayer warriors? Here are three areas that inform intercessors:

1. *"News"*—what's happening in your family and ministry? Tell stories of the people you are reaching.
2. *"Numbers"*—share specifics about your results.
3. *"Needs"*—share your personal and ministry needs. If they don't know what you need, they can't pray for specific answers!

Prayer Strategies

"My Most Wanted" Intercession List
These are the people Jesus has given me a burden to pray for, listen to, serve willingly and share graciously with so they might come to know Him, too.

1.

2.

3.

4.

5.

6.

7.

8.

9.

10.

And also these...

How To "B*L*E*S*S" Others in Prayer

When we pray for God's Kingdom to come, we are asking the Lord to work in people's lives in such a way that they recognize His powerful love drawing them to know Him. As you take time to get to know people and listen for their needs, the Lord will give you wisdom and authority to pray for them. Ask the Lord to "bless" people in the following ways:

Body—*their physical needs (health issues, addictions, etc.)*

Labors—their work (workplace relationships, job needs)

Emotions—their "felt" needs for love, peace, faith, hope

Social—their relationships with family, friends, neighbors and coworkers.

Spiritual—God's best for their lives—His forgiveness, peace, power and a home in Heaven.

Statistical Insights

What do demographic statistics tell you about your mission field in the following areas?

Ethnic diversity—What are the different ethnic groups represented? Who are the majority group or groups? Who are the minority groups? How many languages are spoken? How has the population changed over the past ten years in terms of numbers and ethnicity? What are the projections for the next ten years?

Economic issues—What is the median income and income range in your area? How would your area be described in terms of income and lifestyles?

Employment—What are the different kinds of employment in the area? Who are the major employers? What is the mixture of "white collar," "blue collar" and "no collar" (information and technology) jobs in your area? What is the unemployment rate? How far do people drive to go to work?

Educational—What are the different schools in the area? What is the average level of education?

Entertainment—What kind of entertainment businesses are there? How many of them are harmful to healthy families and communities? Where and how do people spend their money? What kind of recreation facilities are in the area?

"Environment"—How will ministry in this area be affected by local geography, politics and social attitudes?

Family make up—How many are married? Single? What percentage of people fit into the different ages and stages of life (such as children, teens, young adults, senior citizens, etc.)? How many single parent families are there?

Churches—What kinds of churches or spiritual centers of other religions are in the area? What does that tell you?

As you further review the demographic information, what are other insights you should note? Ask the Holy Spirit to point out what He wants you to focus on.

After you review these initial demographic findings, what are your impressions about the kinds of churches and ministries are needed for people in your area?

Spiritual Dynamics

As you "map" your mission field, exegete the culture (which some simply define as "the way we do things around here") from two key perspectives:

First, what are the good qualities of this culture that we can use as bridges for the Good News?

Second, what are the qualities of this culture corrupted by sin that are barriers we must overcome?

Here are some important issues for seeking discernment while doing your spiritual survey work.

1. **Pray!** Ask God to give you understanding of the strongholds of the enemy, the needs of the people and the redemptive possibilities He has in mind.

2. Review the **past.** As you understand the history of your area, you can begin to discern the spiritual influences at work. What important events have taken place? Who were the pioneers of the area? What were their intentions and priorities for this area? What attitudes and behaviors have long been part of the culture?

3. Look at significant **places.** Pay attention to the houses, yards, decorations, signs, businesses and public spaces. How well do people take care of things? Look for monuments, the layout of the area, statues, spiritual places...anything that might help you identify spiritual influences and idols.

4. Look for the seats of **power.** Get to know the government, business, education and religion centers. Who are the key people in positions of power in the area? What are their attitudes toward the things of God? Some communities are highly resistant to God's work. Others (sometimes even literally in a different part of a city or across a geographic boundary) are open and receptive to the Lord. Seek to discern the reasons for those attitudes.

5. What are the **practices** of the community? What are the main festivals or celebrations? What types of activities do many people participate in? What brings people together? What divides them? Pay attention to sports and recreation leagues,

community groups, niche groups, etc. These help us understand the values and priorities of the people in your mission field.

6. Learn about the spiritual **problems** you need to address. What kinds of influence are there from other religions, cults or occult groups? What holds people back from finding God? Find out what people believe in your area. *Learn to listen for people's longings...that's where we are really hearing them on their heart level.*

7. Listen to, link with and pray with your Kingdom **partners**. What other churches are in the area? What is the spiritual condition of other churches? How is the spiritual unity among pastors? What issues do they feel hinder the work of the Kingdom in their area? Find your team mates, ask for their blessing as you join God's team in your area and pray with them!

Spiritual strongholds

Redemptive gifts

Check the S*o*l*L

Key missional questions
- What needs does Jesus want us to meet to bring more people to know Him?
- What assets and relationships could the Lord use redemptively?
- Who knows what we need to know?
- What's not being done in our area that we could do?
- Who are the "persons of peace"?
- What could be our Kingdom niche and unique contribution to His work in this area?

Spheres of Influence Leaders (S*o*l*L)
1. *Education*—school leaders
2. *Law Enforcement*—police chief, sheriff, etc.
3. *Government*—mayor, city/county officials, city planners, etc.
4. *Spiritual leaders*—pastors and parachurch leaders...our Kingdom teammates
5. *Business leaders*—Chamber of Commerce, Rotary, etc.
6. *Social service agencies*
7. *Media*—publishers, radio/TV, etc.
8. *Subcultures*—leaders in niche groups like partiers, bikers, ethnic groups, etc.
9. *Realtors and builders*
10. *"Community organizations"*— groups of people who meet because of a common interest such as Chamber of Commerce, Rotary, support groups, hobbies or other special interests
11. *Sports and recreation organizations*
12. The *"Bishop"*—the most influential spiritual leader of the area to learn from
13. *"Divine appointments"*—watch for the people God sends to you
14. "Niche" groups who may be unique to your area

<u>Survey</u>
1. How would you describe this area to a new person just moving in? What are our greatest strengths?
2. From your position as a leader of influence in this area, what do you see to be our biggest needs?
3. What are some ways a church that wants to be a servant to our area could partner with agencies like yours to help others?
4. What advice would you give me as a new spiritual leader in our community?
5. Who else would you recommend that I talk to who could help me learn more?
6. How can I pray for you or your family? How can we serve you?
7. Thank you for your time! May we keep you updated on our progress?

After you've done your "Check the S*O*I*L" interviews, bring your team together and pray about what you've learned. Glean the key issues from those conversations as indicators of how the Lord is leading you to engage your community redemptively.

Ministry Focus Group Profile

Interests and Free Time	Values and Beliefs
Jobs and Careers	Personal and Community Distinctives

Ministry Audit

Ministries that Go Deep
with God
(Spiritual Formation)

Ministries that Go Deep
with Others
(Authentic Community)

Ministries that Go Deep
Into the Harvest
(Missional Engagement)

Ministries Our
Community Needs
(Missional Possibilities)

Mission and Ministry Teams

Mission Teams	**Ministry Teams**
Developed from study of our mission field	Developed from study of our church's health
Designed to release redemptive gifts to community	Designed to release gifts, skills and passion of Body
Dedicated to ministry Opportunities	Done mainly inside of church
Done mainly outside of church	Discerns opportunities for missional expression

"Living Sent: Developing a Missional Lifestyle"
The "B*E*L*LS" Approach

Michael Frost, in his book *Exiles*, shares a simple but very effective approach to living a more intentional lifestyle, or "missional rhythm," using the acronym B*E*L*L*S. Here's an adaptation:

> "Sanctify them by Your truth, Your word is truth. As You have sent Me into the world, I have sent them into the world." (John 17:17-18, NIV)

> "I will bless you...and you will be a blessing...and in you all the families of the earth will be blessed." (Genesis 12:2,3)

> "So here's what I want you to do, God helping you: Take your everyday, ordinary life—your sleeping, eating, going-to-work and walking-around life—and place it before God as an offering. Romans 12:1-2 (The Message)

Bless at least 3 people each week
*This can be done many ways, but the key is to be intentional. "Blessing" could be an e-mail of affirmation or encouragement, mowing a neighbor's lawn or babysitting for a single mom. It could be a small gift, an act of service or acting as an agent of peace. Bless a person who is a believer. Bless a person who is not a professing Christian. As you've already been using the "B*L*E*S*S" strategy as you pray for people (see our section on intercession), you are now demonstrating God's love in practical ways intentionally.*

Eat with at least 3 other people each week
Eat with a person who is a believer. Eat with a person who is not a professing Christian. Leverage your meal times or coffee breaks for relational investment.

Listen to the promptings of God
Commit to specific times of solitude for active listening to God. Find the ways that you best connect to the Lord and hear His voice.

Make it a part of your daily rhythm, especially in the "spaces" during your day. Give at least one hour each week for this activity.

Learn from the Gospels each week
Read the whole Bible...learn God's story! Have regular rhythm of Bible study. However, take time to specifically read the Gospels in order to learn specifically from Jesus' ways and words.

Share Story
As we spend time with people, we will learn their stories. In their stories we will learn the keys to their hearts and discern how God is working in their lives. Wisely share your own story in ways that connects to their story. Weave in the Good News of God's Story as the Spirit leads. Learn a simple, clear way to present the Gospel so people can respond to the invitation of Jesus to follow Him.

At the end of your day, reflect these two questions...make them a matter of prayer...share them with your accountability partners: In what ways did I cooperate with Jesus today? In what ways did I resist Jesus today?

Missional Calendar

Be intentional about developing *attractional*, *incarnational* and *invitational* ministry. Be sensitive to "receptive" and aware of the "resistant" times on the calendar of people's lives. Churches don't always have to plan events to get people to come to them, we can go where people already are and demonstrate God's love in practical ways there! *"Where people congregate, we will operate."*

"Church" Calendar
Spiritual holidays, especially Christmas and Easter, are still times of the year when many unchurched people are open to coming to church.

"Culture" Calendar
Secular special days Consider Super Bowl Sunday, Valentine's Day, St. Patrick's Day, Mother's Day, Father's Day, July 4th, Canada Day, Halloween and Thanksgiving as spiritual harvest opportunities.

"Community" Calendar
Community festivals
Area schools
City park and recreation departments
Hunting/fishing seasons
Business events

"Celebration/Crisis" Calendar
People are more spiritually accessible in times of transition in their lives. Pay attention to birth, marriage or death announcements, those going through divorce or grief, people who have recently moved, people dealing with addiction.

"Circumstance" Calendar
Occasionally things happen that are not on any of the other calendars we've mentioned. There may be opportunities for churches to team up for special events in their area. It's a powerful witness to people outside the church to see different churches working together as God's team! Churches need to be ready to mobilize their efforts quickly to make the most of these circumstances for bringing Good News to people.

If you are planting a church, be especially sensitive and intentional about launching in a receptive season of your community's calendar. Often this is in the springtime leading up to Easter and in the fall as school begins, but pay attention to the unique dynamics of your local mission field.

Developing Missional Bridges

Ministry activities require effort to become missional bridges. Always plan how you will leverage an activity to build bridges to Jesus and into your church. *Plan each event with the next one in mind.* The more bridges we build for people, the more who will cross over into life in Christ, fruitful relationships with others and meaningful ministry. A ministry out in the community should bridge to one at your church.

Here are some ways to create "missional bridges":

"Taste and See" Plan small and large group opportunities for people to get to know you and your church's vision, values and mission. Let them "taste and see that the Lord is good... and our church is, too!"

"Go and Serve" Go out (sometimes partnering with other community groups) to serve redemptively, demonstrating God's love in practical ways. This is where to deploy your ministry and mission teams. Remember, "Where people congregate, we will operate."

"Learn and Grow" Develop short term seminars or groups to meet felt needs, usually four to six weeks long. These groups can meet inside or outside your church.

"Get to Know" Develop creative ways for people to connect relationally. "Social" can be "spiritual" too! People want to experience life in community. As we do life together, we can see grace at work in each other.

These strategies do not need to be done sequentially. It's more important that they be done sensitively in order to leverage them for building ministry momentum. The key is always being intentional about the relationships they make possible.

As you develop your missional strategy in terms of who you will serve and who you will serve with, give yourself flexibility for "missional discovery." Experiment and field test to see what works and what doesn't. See where the Lord is blessing and join Him. Don't be afraid to change where you devote your missional energy.

Strategy from an Acts 1:8 Perspective

Beyond our initial Ministry Focus Group (see "Jerusalem"), the Lord wants us to pay attention to other opportunities He's preparing. Using Acts 1:8 as a missional grid, prayerfully consider new possibilities to spread grace to new places. Who are the people your local church has the greatest potential to impact for Christ?

Jerusalem—People **near** us and **like** us. They will come to our church as we will find ways to build redemptive bridges to them. Describe them...

Judea—People **like** us, but not **near** us. They would come to our church, but are too far away. What kinds of ministries or another church could we start to reach them where they live? What possibilities and locations come to mind?

Samaria—People **near** us, but not **like** us. They may not connect easily to our church, but we could start another ministry, service or church for them even though it's close to our own church. What people groups or special opportunities might fit "Samaria" ministry?

Ends of the earth—People not **like** us and not **near** us. Increasingly, ministry is blending local and global to become "glocal." Consider how you can partner with missionaries in other parts of the world to plant churches and other missional initiatives. Work with your denomination's global missions team to discover what opportunities might fit your church.

Listening to Their Story...Sharing Your Story and God's Story

Listen for the Longings in Their Story...
Here's a "Top Ten List" that describes what the lost are looking for from us as Christians...

10. I don't care how much you know until I know how much you care.

9. Have compassion on me. Don't condemn me because my life's a mess.

8. Ask "permission" to tell me about God, don't just push Him on me. Talk *with* me, not *at* me. Listen to me. Find out about my world before you expect me to be interested in yours.

7. Use words I can understand.

6. Have a sense of humor! I want Christianity that can be enjoyed, not endured.

5. Don't focus on your church. Labels don't mean much to me. I'm looking for people who live like they really love God. Chances are I've been burnt or bored in church situations in the past.

4. Don't just tell me about your faith, show me your faith by serving others in love.

3. Take your time. Don't tell me everything at once. Give me time to let God work in my life.

2. Tell me how God can make a difference in my daily life, not just at church on Sunday. If I'm going to be a Christian, I want it to work in real life.

1. Make Jesus real to me. Show me simply how to know Him from His Word and chances are I'll want to know Him, too. After all, I really do want to go to Heaven.

Share Your Story...and God's Story

Before I met Jesus, my life was....

I realized I needed Jesus when.....

I committed my life to Jesus by....

Since I met Jesus my life is.....

You can know Jesus, too, by.....

Discovery Bible Study

Discovery Bible Study Priorities
1. Start with a Person of Peace (Luke 10:6)

2. Seek to lead a person/family/group to discover God and His salvation. Our goal is transformed people through obedience and promised based discipleship!

3. The Scripture is the authority. Lead a simple inductive Bible Study each week.

4. Group Interaction

Discovery Bible Study --Connecting Relationally
*Accountability
> Ask: What are you thankful for this week? (Prayer)
> Ask: What needs do you or others have? (Intercession)
> Ask: How can we help meet the needs expressed? (Ministry)

* Bible Study
> Ask: With whom did you share last week's lesson? (Evangelism)
> Ask: How did you apply what you learned last week? (Obedience)

The Discovery Bible Study Process—Connecting to God's World

1st Pass: Read the Scripture Text
- What did you like most about this passage?
- What did you find difficult or confusing in this passage?

2nd Pass: Read the Passage Again
- What does this passage teach us about God?
- What does this teach us about ourselves?

3rd Pass: Ask someone to retell the story or passage.
- If this is true, how would we have to obey? What does God want you to do about it? What promise do you see about how God will help you obey?
- Who can you share what you just learned with?

For pre-believers you can start with Creation and work through the Bible to Christ, focusing on the attributes of God. For new believers you will start with commands of Christ

Focus on the Scripture, not human opinion...trust the Holy Spirit!

(Adapted from: Discovery Bible Study, David Watson. Get further information at: http://e3partners.org/resources /learning-resources/)

Ministry Timeline and Flow Chart

A <u>ministry flow chart</u> is a diagram of major ministries, programs, teams and events.

- It shows each ministry in relation to the others.
- It shows the logical sequence by which people become connected and involved step by step.
- It shows the intended result of ministry involvement.
- It is useful to show what ministries might be missing, especially missional teams.
- It shows how your missional game plan begins out in your mission field, makes disciples and then deploys disciples and teams back into your mission field!
- It has missional multiplication in mind!

1. List each major ministry team, event or program that you currently have or plan to have on a Post-it® note. If you are starting a new service, ministry or church, plan with your intended outcome in mind.

2. Organize the Post-it® notes in a pathway on a poster board to show how you will connect to unchurched people, lead them to Christ, grow them in leadership and equip them as a reproducing leader. Make sure you can see an intentional disciple-making pathway.

3. If designing a new ministry (or church), put dates on the pathway so it also becomes a timeline. Although you are more "checkpoint" than calendar driven in your planning, set a date in the future for the new ministry to begin and work backward from this launch date to establish the sequence necessary for a successful launch.

4. Review your work as a team. Identify any missing essential ministries, teams or events. Add them in.

5. Identify any unnecessary ministry activities and set them aside. Look for "bottlenecks and disconnects"—points where progress can easily be interrupted or hindered. Think about what level of commitment is required to be involved at each ministry step. What additional strategies might be needed to

grow and equip people at each step? What communication and relationships are needed to move people from one level of commitment and involvement to another?

6. Now connect the Post-it® notes with arrows to form a pathway and timeline for your game plan. Give yourself permission to adapt your plan as situations warrant. Put everything at the disposal and direction of the Holy Spirit. Dream big. Work hard. Stay dependent. Pray much. Expect! Developing a game plan for missional ministry is one of the most rewarding things you can do...cover everything with prayer, keep at it...and watch God work through you!

The Secret Church Shopper Survey
Alan Nelson, Stan Toler, Priscilla Hammond, Tim Roehl

Our goal: to get a picture of how a church "looks" to new people... strengths to celebrate, weaknesses to address.

Media
_____ Website (easy to navigate, clear information, sensitive to guests, attractive, etc.)
_____ Social media (Facebook, Twitter, etc.)

Facilities
_____ Parking (ease, accessibility, signage)
_____ Ease in determining main entrance
_____ Landscaping
_____ Ease in finding the church
_____ Exterior signs (condition, clarity, size)
_____ Exterior of facility and church buildings (paint, curb appeal)
_____ Signage/maps to help me find where I need to go once inside
_____ Temperature
_____ Accessibility (aisles, space between rows, handicapped accessible)
_____ Open spaces for gathering, greeting, people flow (do people block entrances?)

Hospitality
_____ Greeting (by anyone, warmly/coolly, too gregarious.
     Did I feel overlooked? Overwhelmed?)
_____ Offered help in finding location/classroom
_____ Appearance of greeters
_____ Visible name badges
_____ Offered bulletin/worship folder
_____ Knowledgeable of facility/class locations/church information
_____ Refreshments
_____ Did I feel comfortable as a newcomer, or under a spotlight?

Nursery
_____ Signage/directions
_____ Cleanliness
_____ Staff (adequate number, competence, appearance)

_____ Facility (size, appearance, equipment)
_____ Check-in system
_____ Security
_____ Check-out system
_____ Pager system

Children's Ministry
_____ Teacher there/semblance of order
_____ I met the teacher
_____ Child was greeted, made to feel at home
_____ Directions to classroom
_____ Introduction/orientation
_____ Equipment
_____ Decorations
_____ Take-home materials
_____ Check-in system
_____ Check-out system
_____ Follow-up

Youth
_____ Teacher there/semblance of order
_____ I met the teacher
_____ Child was greeted, made to feel at home
_____ Directions to classroom
_____ Introduction/orientation
_____ Lesson
_____ Equipment
_____ Decorations
_____ Follow-up

Worship Service
_____ Arrival time _____
_____ Friendliness (general feel, warmth)
_____ Auditorium appearance
_____ Seating (availability, comfort)
_____ Help offered to find seat
_____ Audio (soft, loud, quality)
_____ Could I see the screen?

____ Worship Leader and Team
- Was the music balanced (vocal versus instruments)?
- Outwardly focused on congregation (eyes open and connecting with people)
- Authentic, genuine worship
- Connecting with God (not performance oriented)
- Song selection (fits the theme and feel of the service, singable)
- Transitions (between songs and from worship to prayer or announcements)
- Demographics (diverse?)

____ Did the worship service flow freely?

____ Message/sermon
    ____ Length
    ____ Clarity
    ____ Interest
    ____ Relevance
    ____ Notes
    ____ Energy level
    ____ Pastoral perceptions (attire, friendliness, etc.)
    ____ Content (Biblical and practical)

____ Left understanding theme of the service?

____ Length of service

____ Relevance (contemporary, liturgical, traditional flavor)

____ Did I feel informed about what I was to do/when? How sensitive were they to visitors/guests?

Rest Rooms
____ Signage/directions
____ Lighting
____ Décor
____ Aroma
____ Cleanliness

Visual Image Package
____ Bulletin/worship folder (printing, graphics, clarity, information)
____ Newsletter
____ Brochures
____ Business card

_____ Advertising
_____ Logo
_____ Signage
_____ Foyer area
_____ Information availability (arrangement, thoroughness, appeal)

Follow-Up
_____ Appropriate amount (too much, too little)
_____ Type of follow-up received
_____ Overall comfort (embarrassed, felt welcome, etc.)
_____ Friendliness of people
_____ Friendliness of pastor/staff

Miscellaneous Survey Possibilities
_____ Called the church for information and was received well
_____ Requests were followed-up by appropriate staff
_____ Received the information by mail or email in _____ days
_____ How is the church perceived in the community?
_____ What are our strengths, weaknesses?
_____ Is this a place where you would want to return? Why or why not?
_____ Is this a place where you would invite your friends/neighbors to attend? Why or why not?

Adapted by Tim Roehl and Priscilla Hammond from *The Five-Star Church*, © 1999 by Stan Toler and Alan Nelson

Appendix D
"Spy Teams" To Help You Discern God's Missional Game Plan for Your Church

As you seek to discern God's vision, values and mission for your church, a great strategy is to "spy out the land" to see where God is at work and join Him. Your mission is to ask questions, listen carefully, discern the lessons prayerfully and develop plans strategically.

The "History" Team—Looking Back

Why is it important to review your church's history? There are several important reasons...

It gives *perspective*. You'll understand better...
- why your church was <u>planted</u>
- who the <u>pioneers</u>/heroes were who took the risk to obey God
- what <u>priorities</u> motivated them
- what <u>problems</u> they faced and overcame
- what <u>promises</u> God gave them to help trust Him
- what <u>plans</u> they prayed through and made in the church's early days

It gives *permission*. We often gain permission for our future from the lessons of our past! What risk taking faith and obedience did your church's forefathers demonstrate that you can emulate today?

Key Questions for the "History" Team

1. Why did your church begin? Who were the pioneers/risk takers for God? How did your church begin? What were significant factors in your church's beginning? What can you learn from them?

2. When were your church's "glory days?" What did they look like? What was God doing in your midst? How did your people respond? What can you learn from them?

3. When were some of your church's "groaning days" when you went through difficult or lean times? What was happening? What were the factors that led to those times? What can you learn from them?

4. As you look at your church's potential and problems today, ask yourself, "Given the decisions they made then, what do we think those pioneers would have done with this issue?"

The "Community" Team—Looking Around

Why is important to see what is happening in your community?

It helps us discern the *"spiritual climate"* of your area. It is vital to see the big picture of what God is doing in your region in order to best find your place on God's Kingdom team. What are the "besetting sins" of your area—areas of visible pain and spiritual captivity? These often show us God's "redemptive opportunities" for ministry.

It helps you find the *"persons of peace"* in your area. They are the people who have significant influence with numbers of people. Sometimes they have positions of formal power. Some may be "informal" leaders without title but with great wisdom and influence. Learning from them and gaining their favor is vital, often opening whole networks of people you can serve for Christ.

It helps you discern your *"opportunities and obstacles"* as you seek to reach others for Christ. What strongholds of sin hold people back from knowing Jesus? What redemptive gifts does Jesus want to release to set people free? What needs can you meet? What kinds of people aren't being reached? What "open doors" can you discover for ministry?

Key Questions for the "Community" Team

What can you learn as you check the "S*o*I*L"... (Sphere of Influence Leaders) in your community?
Develop a list and set up appointments with key leaders in various spheres of influence such as:

a. *Education*—school leaders.
b. *Law Enforcement*—police chief, sheriff, etc.
c. *Government*—mayor, city/county officials, city planners, etc.
d. *Spiritual leaders*—pastors and parachurch leaders...our Kingdom teammates.
e. *Business leaders*—Chamber of Commerce, Rotary, etc.
f. *Social service agencies.*
g. *Media*—publishers, radio/TV, etc.
h. *Subcultures*—leaders in niche groups like partiers, bikers, ethnic groups, etc.
i. *Realtors and builders.*
j. *"People of peace"*—those who have influence in the area whether they have a "title" or not and can open doors to large networks of relationships. Other leaders may tell you talk to them. They may have lived in your area for a long time and seen the changes the community has gone through.
k. The *"Bishop"*—the most influential spiritual leader of the area to learn from and get his blessing.
l. *"Divine appointments"*—watch for the people God sends to you!

Here's a sample survey you can use with these "sphere of influence" leaders. Remember, be gracious and be brief. If they appear interested and want to give you more time, take advantage of their generosity and learn much.

1. How would you describe this area to a new person just moving in? What are the greatest strengths?

2. From your position as a leader of influence in this area, what do you see to be the biggest needs?

3. What are some ways a church that wants to be a servant to our area could partner with agencies like yours to help others?

4. What advice would you give me as a new spiritual leader in our community?

5. Who else would you recommend that I talk to who could help me learn more?

6. How can I pray for you and your family? How can we serve you?

7. Thank you for your time! May we keep you updated on our progress?

What kind of people groups live in your area? Who are you best suited to reach for Christ? (Ministry Focus Group) Who is reaching them for Christ? Ask, "How would we design our ministry if we were to take this people group seriously?"

The "Congregational" Team—Looking Within

An excellent resource to help you better discern your church's strengths is the "Natural Church Development" (NCD) tool. Let your NCD scores and materials serve as a reference point and a ministry resource for you. Make sure your prayer warriors are saturating everything with prayer!

Key Questions for the "Congregational" Team

1. What dreams and expectations do the people of your church have for your ministry? How can you connect individual dreams with the bigger vision of your church?

2. What gifts do you see among the people of your church? How can they best be utilized to reach the lost and build up the Body of Christ?

3. What are your church's greatest strengths? How can you leverage them to reach more people?

4. Look over your church's facilities. What changes may be needed in order to best serve the people God has called you to reach?

5. What new ministries may be needed to help you accomplish the vision God is giving you?

6. What trends are you noticing in your church? What can you learn from them? How could you address them most wisely?

The "Kingdom" Team—Looking at God's Team

Your church is only one part of the "Kingdom Team" of churches and leaders God is raising up to reach your area for Christ. By learning what He is doing in other churches and ministries you can best discern His Kingdom niche for your church.

Have members of this team visit other churches in your area and talk with the leaders of those churches.

Key Questions for the "Kingdom" Team

1. What are some of your general observations about the health of the other ministries in your area? What are they doing that is having the biggest impact for Christ?

2. What needs are not being met by the other ministries in your area that your church could seek to provide?

3. How can you partner with other ministries in your area to make the most impact for the Lord?

4. How can you bless other ministries in your area?

Bringing It All Together...

After all the Spy Teams have "scouted out the land," come back together and have each share their findings. List them on Post-it® Pads across a wall in this order...

History   Congregational   Community   Kingdom

As each Spy Team shares their findings, have the whole group summarize the main insights.

Then, review again the findings of the Congregational and Community Spy Teams. What connections can you see between who you are as a church and what needs/opportunities in your community you might be able to address in Jesus' name? What ministries might you develop to meet those needs and bring people to Christ?

In light of what you have learned and discerned from "scouting out the land," what are the next steps you can take as a church? Make some clear action steps stated as S*M*A*R*T goals:

Specific
Measureable
Achievable
Relevant
Time bound

You may want to find a good ministry coach to help you as you take your next steps...a good coach is an invaluable resource!

Remember...your mission field is your "Promised Land" ...God is leading you...go take the land!

OMS · ONE MISSION SOCIETY

By God's grace, One Mission Society unites, inspires, and equips Christians to make disciples of Jesus Christ, multiplying dynamic communities of believers around the world.

One Mission Society is an evangelical, interdenominational faith mission that makes disciples of Jesus Christ through intentional evangelism, planting churches, and training national leaders In Africa, Asia, the Caribbean, Europe, and Latin America. One Mission Society then joins with those churches in global partnerships to reach the rest of the world.

One Mission Society
PO Box A
Greenwood, IN 46142
317.888.3333
www.onemissionsociety.org

Made in the USA
Charleston, SC
16 May 2016